In North Korea

In North Korea

*An American Travels
Through an
Imprisoned Nation*

NANCHU *with* XING HANG

McFarland & Company, Inc., Publishers
Jefferson, North Carolina, and London

*We would like to thank Mr. Zhongyi Wu
and Ms. Elizabeth Frost-Knappman
for their contribution to this book.*

Photographs are by the author unless credited otherwise

LIBRARY OF CONGRESS CATALOGUING-IN-PUBLICATION DATA

Nanchu, 1953–
    In North Korea : an American travels through an imprisoned
nation / Nanchu with Xing Hang.
        p.   cm.
    Includes index.

    ISBN 0-7864-1691-2 (softcover : 50# alkaline paper) ∞

    1. Korea (North)—Description and travel.   2. Korea (North)—
Social conditions.   I. Hang, Xing, 1982–   II. Title.
    DS932.4.N36   2003
    951.9304'3 — dc21   2003010988

British Library cataloguing data are available

On the cover: foreground— statue of Kim Il Sung in downtown
Pyongyang; *background—* Tumen River

Manufactured in the United States of America

*McFarland & Company, Inc., Publishers
  Box 611, Jefferson, North Carolina 28640
  www.mcfarlandpub.com*

Injustice anywhere is a threat to justice everywhere.

—*Martin Luther King, Jr.*
"Letter from the Birmingham Jail," 1963

Contents

Preface

To me, the great famine unfolding in North Korea in the early 2000s is like a nightmare constantly replaying, reminding me of the tragic childhood I spent in the three-year, man-made famine caused by Mao Zedong's Great Leap Forward Program, a political movement designed to beat the Western world, to prove the superiority of communism over capitalism. Dreaming of changing China from an agricultural country to an industrial one overnight, Mao ordered the peasants to put down their hoes and set up shabby furnaces to produce iron.

In those days in China, everyone made steel, but the fertile farmland became deserted. For three years, no good harvests were realized. The entire nation starved. Markets had nothing to sell. Rations were cut or in the rural areas stopped entirely. Without much to eat, my stomach grew numb, not feeling hunger at all even though I had become reduced to a bag of bones.

Today, the North Korean people's diet of grass roots and tree bark painfully reminds me of the daily diet that my family once had. The human body cannot digest this kind of food, which causes inner bleeding and severe diarrhea. Several of my relatives in the rural areas did not survive. One desperate uncle chewed dirt and was bloated to death. Another went to the fields to dig wild vegetables. He died of poisoning.

I grew up under the brutality of Mao's rule. Even though I became one of his Red Guard leaders and one of his notorious worker-peasant-soldier college students, I always lived with unspeakable fear, never knowing when I would become his revolutionary target. Persecution was as close as a slight slip of tongue.

Mao's "proletarian dictatorship" and communist utopia produced nothing but poverty and one disaster after another for the Chinese people. Eating from the "socialist iron bowl," they were so poor that Khrushchev once offered this vivid description of their lives: "They drink clear water from a big pot, and five farmers share one pair of pants if they have to go out."

The example of the loss of millions of Chinese lives has not taught the leader of neighboring North Korea, Kim Jong Il, a lesson. Today, the man-made famine in North Korea has already starved millions. The mortality rate rises rapidly and silently right under our noses. Having lived the good life in the United States, I could find it easy to become a passive spectator. Nevertheless, I am a living witness, victim and survivor of a similarly fatal famine and the brutality of an equally evil dictator. Many people in the United States may think that what has happened to people in faraway North Korea has nothing to do with them. However, in today's globalized world, North Korea has become our next-door neighbor. What Robert Kennedy once said still rings true: "If one man's right is violated, the rights of all are endangered."

I went to North Korea in 2001 and kept a careful diary. The trip to North Korea was dangerous because of the strong anti–American feelings there: If my American citizenship had been discovered, I might not have come out of the country.

The moment I entered North Korea, the gnawing fear I felt living under Mao overwhelmed me again and immediately took me back to those tragic days. I felt sick at my stomach during the entire trip. But I put on a brave front for self-protection, since even fear itself is a crime in countries like North Korea.

The North Korean government not only tries to hide its grim reality from other nations; it has also deceived its own people about the famine, the deaths, and the views of China, South Korea, and the outside world. It has tried to block any external influence on the country. Free movement in North Korea is impossible and finding the truth very difficult. However, my coauthor, Xing Hang, a brave young scholar from the University of Georgia, took a separate trip to North Korea to confirm my observations, collect new information, and help me with interviews and research in Yanbian Korean Autonomous Prefecture in China. Together with him, I finally found my voice in this book. Though the book may not be perfect, the information we gathered, both firsthand and secondhand, opens a small window and allows the reader to take a look into the secret land of Kim Jong Il. It is our hope that the book makes the bitter cries of the North Korean people heard.

The truth about the communist dictators who live in the dark shadows has always been hard to get. Mao's famine became known only years after his death. Today, the world need not and should not have to wait passively for the passing of Kim Jong Il in order to find out the truth about his secret kingdom.

Nanchu
June 2003

PART I

A Country in Prison

1. The Yalu River

It is a bright afternoon in June 2000. I stand by the Yalu River, which separates the Chinese port of Dandong from her North Korean counterpart, Sinuiju. The reflection from the sun dances with the rippling water. With thousands of twists and turns, the Yalu River passes green hills and towering mountains, emptying into the Bo Hai Sea at the end of its journey.

As I gaze across the river into North Korea, images flash through my mind.

North Korean women crawl in the fields, digging into the ground for grass roots. Small children on their backs cry for a bite to eat. Bigger ones stand beside their mothers, their arms and legs like dry twigs.

Young girls sell blood for food. At night, they risk their lives raiding grain trains. Teenage boys climb over mountains and wade through swift streams, running to the Sino-Korean border. They say that they want to see the world before they die.

Ragged men looking for food climb onto the tops of trains to get a ride, refusing to get down even at gunpoint. The high-voltage wire runs just inches above their heads.

At the train station, passengers sell their clothes for something to eat. There, those who are alive one second drop dead the next.

The bare farmland. Mile after mile of rusting factories. Hungry adults on the furrowed dirt roads. Hollow-eyed children tightly holding empty rice bowls. A famine mankind has rarely seen before unfolds silently in North Korea.

I board a sightseeing boat and cruise around the damaged Yalu Bridge.

The Yalu International Bridge.

During the Korean War, the Americans bombed the Korean side of the structure to stop incoming transportation from China. It has never been rebuilt since. Left only are the concrete base columns standing lonely in the water, reminding people of one of the cruelest wars in modern history.

Since the Yalu River has no boundary line and can be used by both countries, the boat travels close to the North Korean shore. Twenty meters away from the shore stands a lonely, huge white house with black flying roofs and flaking paint. This is the biggest restaurant in Sinuiju; its front door is closed and no customers go in or out. Among the trees, a huge portrait of Kim Il Sung colors the gray streets. Gigantic political banners mounted on top of the apartment buildings proclaim the socialist victory. On the beach, an old wooden boat rests upside down. A group of men in faded gray and brown uniforms surround it, apparently holding an inspection discussion. Their hands are behind their backs. No one has any tools. On the bank, soldiers patrol behind them. In the river, a few skinny boys play with the water, smiling and waving at us. The tourists hurl cookies and candies back at them. Our cruiser passes a rustic ship sitting on the beach. The vessel uses the sands as a natural dock, because the North Koreans lack modern harbor facilities. Two soldiers guard the gaunt-looking cargo crew as they unload the heavy grain sacks on board. A chilling gleam catches my attention. It is from the bayonets pointed at the workers. I shiver. The blood seems to have stopped running within me.

Since the early 1990s, North Korea has suffered from a massive famine. In the Chinese city of Dandong behind me, many Victory-brand trucks roam the streets. These old, blue North Korean vehicles, imported from the Soviet Union during the 1950's, are laden with sacks of grain. China is one of the world's leading food suppliers to North Korea during its prolonged famine, and Dandong is the chief port from which relief goods are shipped.

My family used to live in Northeast China in the 1960s. Dandong then was a remote, desolate border city lacking even the most essential necessities such as cooking oil, sugar, and soap. But now, at the turn of the new millennium, it has become a regional economic powerhouse thanks to former leader Deng Xiaoping's reforms during the past twenty years. Overlooking the Yalu River, tall buildings line the banks. Huge billboards promote life insurance, candy, clothing, and electronics, among other things. Shining cars and new bicycles fill the streets. In the past, the people of Dandong could eat only rationed corn, millet, and sorghum. Wheat and rice were luxuries available only on national holidays. But today, countless restaurants have opened. Markets overflow with various kinds of agricultural products coming from as far as Guangdong province, in the southern end of China. After dusk, residents stroll on the streets, dancing and singing karaoke, shopping in the night market, and enjoying local delicacies from the food peddlers lining the streets.

Dandong is a sleepless city full of vigor.

However, just a few hundred meters away, Sinuiju, also a big border city like Dandong, lies deadly quiet in the pitch darkness. Even in daylight, only a small handful of pedestrians move slowly on the empty streets, which have no cars, no buses, not even bicycles. The apartment buildings look old and poor. Families share rooms and toilets. Most windows have no glass. They are just holes, big holes. Only a few are covered with pieces of torn-up plastic. How residents spend the severe winter, when temperatures drop to thirty degrees below zero, one cannot imagine. Several tin stovetop chimneys jut from the top of these buildings, indicating that people still use coal for cooking and heating. But even those look lifeless; no smoke comes out of them.

A strong desire develops within me to go to the other side of the Yalu River, to find out the truth behind the deadly silence. But how?

North Korea has built a stone fortress and shut itself inside. It is one of the most secluded and secretive places in the world. Outsiders know very little about what lies within. Western journalists are generally banned. Even the movements of reporters from "friendly" countries such as China and Russia are strictly controlled.

China, which enjoys a relationship with North Korea as close as "lips and teeth," is the only country from which North Korea allows travelers in large numbers. In the past few years, the Dandong International Travel Service has organized numerous travel groups visiting North Korea. There are several popular tours, like a one-day trip to Sinuiju or to the Rajin Special Economic Zone. Someone wanting a broader experience could try the four-day trip to Manpo, Mt. Myohyang, Pyongyang, Kaesong, and Panmunjom, near the Demilitarized Zone (DMZ). The warm-hearted Dandong people tell me not to worry if I forget to bring valid credentials. As long as I can pay 3,000 yuan for the trip — quite a lot for an ordinary Chinese — the travel service will "borrow" the documentation for me.

In high spirits, I go to the Dandong International Travel Service, located in a modern building near the train station. A gray-haired man in his fifties greets me. He introduces himself as the president. When I tell him my intention, he shakes his head.

"You are very unlucky," he says. Just a few days ago, North Korea not only closed all its travel routes, but also closed the entire country for the summit meeting between Workers Party Secretary Kim Jong Il and South Korea's president, Kim Dae-jung. No one knows when or if North Korea will reopen itself to foreigners.

The man continues, "We have been actively negotiating with North Korea, persuading it to open more of its cities and to become a formal and regular tourist nation. Let's hope for the best. So many people are curious about what is happening on the other side of the Yalu."

One year later, in 2001, I visit China again. My desire to see North Korea had grown even stronger. The summit talks between the two Koreas are long over, with Kim Dae-jung winning the Nobel Peace Prize as a result. However, all travel routes from Dandong, the largest border city in China, to North Korea remain closed. The Korean side says that it is not ready to open up because it lacks travel facilities such as transportation, hotels, and restaurants. But the real reason could be that it is scared of ideological and cultural invasion of the isolated country. In reality, not only all the routes from Dandong, but also those from other smaller border cities such as Tumen and Yanji, have been shut down.

But I refuse to give up hope. On the Internet, I discover my last chance. Ji'an, on the middle reaches of the Yalu River, is still open. It is not an ideal city, for it hides behind deep mountains and is a dead end, with no major railroads linking it to the big cities. In contrast, Dandong is a transportation hub, with airports and major railways connecting it to Beijing, Shanghai, Dalian, and Harbin.

I immediately contact the Ji'an International Travel Service. The procedure is not as simple as the Dandong people said. On the contrary, it is quite complicated. First, I would have to hand in eight recent passport pictures taken on a blue background. The Korean authorities do not accept photos on white background. (My first batch of pictures was returned to me. The amused photographer said, "I have taken passport pictures for all my life. Don't forget Shanghai is a city with 12 million people. My goodness, this is the first time that I have heard of this. Why is North Korea so fussy about the background color? Which century is it still in?")

Next, the photos have to be sent along with an original picture ID issued by the Chinese government. I fill out an application form providing the North Korean government with information as detailed as what my grandfather did for a living. Having worked on the application for days, I hand in the package for both the Chinese and North Korean authorities to examine. Finally, I receive a phone call from the travel agency telling me that I have passed the political investigation and will join a group that heads out in July.

It is drizzling the day I leave Shanghai. The train travels at 140 kilometers an hour on the major railway trunkline that runs from South to North China. June is the rainy season south of the Yangtze River. In the mist, new farmhouses with glazed pink walls and shining black roofs, webs of rivers and creeks, and rice paddies lined with sweeping willows rush past me. Wet winds blowing into the windows carry the fresh smell of green crops.

After the train crossed the Yangtze River Bridge in Nanjing, Northern China greets me with its dry air and scorching heat. Yellow dust flies everywhere, falling on grass blades, trees, cows, houses…. This year the region is suffering from its most serious drought in decades. The rainfall is 70 percent less than normal years. Huge sandstorms from Inner Mongolia have swallowed the capital, Beijing. Affected farmland is over 3.415 billion hectares. Rivers, wells, and reservoirs have all dried up. On top of all that, the East Asian locusts have invaded the farmlands, covering the ground like a thick blanket. The density of the insects can be as much as 3,000 heads per square meter.[1] Located next to Jilin Province in Northeast China, North Korea is equally affected, suffering from the severest drought in three hundred years, worsening the already acute situation of food shortage.

In the past, if such a serious natural disaster hit, Chinese peasants would have abandoned their homes and run for their lives. Villages would become empty and bodies line the roads. However, not a single peasant starved to death during the 2000–2001 drought. For the first time in history, the Chinese farmers have bid farewell to the old days when this monster could wipe out village after village.

The train roars ahead. The trip takes me almost three days. From Shenyang, the biggest regional hub of the Northeast, I change to a train headed for the Yanbian Korean Autonomous Prefecture, home of China's ethnic Korean minority. Its size is one third that of North Korea. Yanbian, nicknamed "Little South," is a beautiful place with picturesque scenery. Green mountains loom in the distance, and clear water runs in a network of ditches and streams. Peasants whip cattle, plowing the rich fields. The Korean Chinese have successfully grown rice in this cold province for centuries, while the Han majority only planted wheat, corn, millet and sorghum.

It is already dark when I arrive at Tonghua, regional capital of Jilin Province, where I am to change trains to Ji'an. But there is no Ji'an train this late. The earliest one would be next midday and it would take four hours to cover a distance of only 120 kilometers, since the branch railway, built by the Japanese, has not been upgraded since the thirties. Time is urgent. I have to meet my group at 1:00 the next afternoon.

The small northern train station is crowded. The scantily dressed locals surround exhausted travelers, scrambling to offer deals on hotels, taxis, buses, and restaurants.

A young man in a sleeveless sweatshirt grabs my arm.

"Thirty yuan! Thirty yuan to Ji'an!"

"Thirty yuan to Ji'an! Want to go?" The young man urges, stretching out three fingers.

He almost pushes me into his taxi together with two other passengers. With an income of 90 yuan for the night, the young driver is happy: it is worthwhile for him to climb over the steep mountains and make the trip. Our car ascends and descends one peak after another at record speed. Outside, dark objects fly by. All I can see are the deep gorges a long distance below the zigzag, though paved, mountain road. To my surprise, there are villages even in the deep mountains. Very often, I see villagers in twos and threes walking along the highway. Men stride shoulder to shoulder and girls, hand in hand. The young driver casually smokes one cigarette after another while controlling the steering wheel with his free hand.

He points at the valleys enveloped in the darkness.

"Deep down there, we hide our missiles and tanks."

"For what?"

"Those weapons? They target North Korea."

"North Korea?" I am shocked.

"Why?" The other two passengers from Harbin and Beijing are also stunned.

"You guys from the inland may not know. For a long time, we have had a territorial dispute with the North Koreans. They claim that Ji'an is theirs, but of course it is our territory," the young driver exclaims angrily, a typical Chinese showing his strong nationalism.

But North Korea doesn't buy it, he says. It builds defensive systems along the border. He tells us that during the daytime, if we look carefully across the Yalu, we will see their fortresses, lots of them, hidden behind the trees. They constantly deploy their soldiers, preparing for war. "On our side," says the driver, "we have had no good roads going through here before. This one was built just for defensive purposes. The atmosphere is pretty tense here."

I do see many Chinese soldiers in this border area. Some are building trenches through the fields. On the train to Ji'an, a young female officer sitting next to me is from the Second Artillery Troop. She has just come back from intensive technology training in Beijing. Apparently, the relationship between the two brother socialist countries is not as "inseparable as lips and teeth" after all.

Most Koreans, regardless of whether they are from the North or South, consider the Ji'an region as their territory. During ancient times, Ji'an used to be the capital of the Koguryo kingdom. Inside the city, one can still find remains such as city walls, graves, and pyramids left over from that era. At its height, the monarchy included huge portions of what is China's Northeast today. In the 8th century, the kingdom was wiped out by the T'ang Dynasty.

The Koreans believe that the Koguryo people were their ancestors, and the historical remains provide strong evidence that this region belongs to them. But the Chinese have different perspectives. The kingdom of Koguryo, they argue, originated in Hunjiang of China's Liaoning Province. Furthermore, they believe that the Koguryo people were Chinese minorities, rather than members of another nation.

The taxi driver says that in 1962 Chinese Premier Zhou Enlai gave all the islands in the Yalu River to North Korea as a gesture of friendship. But both Koreas continue to dispute other territories along the border, including the 33 kilometers of boundary along Mt. Paektu-san (Changbai Mountains, as the Chinese call it) and the Ji'an area.

Many South Koreans trace their roots back to North Korea. About one in every seven people in both countries has relatives on the other side of the DMZ. However, after the Korean War, all communications were cut between the two Koreas. For South Koreans, the Sino-Korean border is the closest thing they could come to getting a glimpse of the other part of their country.

A front-desk woman in my hotel tells me a tragic story about a former customer, an old South Korean man in his eighties. The man's only wish before he dies is to see his son, from whom he has been separated for more than half a century. Since there is no way he can enter North Korea, the old man came to Ji'an. For days, he lingered at the bank of the Yalu, looking across the River. Then, he disappeared. Later, his body floated onto the water's surface. In the letter he left behind, he wrote, "My dear son, I want to embrace you, but here is the River that I cannot cross. I want to kiss the land you live in, but here is the mountain that I cannot go over...."

In Ji'an, I see a sightseeing boat cruising along the Yalu River: on the side of the deck facing North Korea, South Korean travelers are packed in rows stretching their necks out, searching for any signs of life and activity in the poor villages. Many wipe their eyes, sighing and sobbing. The forbidden land, where members of their own flesh and blood belong, lies so close to them, yet so unapproachable.

2. Slow Train

I arrive at the Ji'an train station on time.

In this small border town, no outlines of tall buildings block the view so the sky looks high and far. Near the station, farmers wearing straw hats stand by their flat carts stacked high with fresh cucumbers, tomatoes, and various kinds of fruits. They hawk at the travelers, "Buy some cucumbers and carry them with you! You won't have any vegetables once in North Korea!"

I wait with 74 other Chinese travelers for departure to the forbidden land. For the year 2001, the North Korean government allows only four tour groups to enter. We are the second one. The majority of the tourists are middle-aged males, usually government officials and leaders of state-owned enterprises. Our group also includes several provincial governors and Supreme Court judges. The cost of the trip is beyond the means of a common Chinese, who earns on the average 500 yuan ($65) a month.

However, not every person in the group is using public money to pay for the expensive trip. A plump woman named Suyi goes along with her parents. She is a private business owner, a Korean Chinese from the Yanbian Korean Autonomous Prefecture. Speaking fluent Chinese, the woman tells me that after China opened up itself during the late eighties, she had spent several years in South Korea doing all kinds of odd jobs that the people there did not want to do. She cleaned houses and office buildings, worked in salons and beauty shops to make money. In the South, she found no cultural barriers. The Korean language spoken in Yanbian, though slightly different from that in South Korea, is well understood. However, Suyi still went back to China after making enough money, which she says will last the rest of her life even if she does not work at all.

"This is my country. You feel comfortable living here with everything you are familiar with. There, you just go and make money." Her uncle, who had fought as a Chinese "volunteer" in the Korean War, was buried in North Korea. She often accompanies her parents to pay a visit to the country for which her uncle died.

Two men in their thirties look mysterious, wearing sunglasses all the time. One of them is bilingual, speaking both Chinese and Korean. I later find out that they are plain clothes Chinese national security personnel on a special mission in North Korea.

Little Wang, a young man in his early twenties, is our Chinese tour guide. Fresh out of college, this is his first time leading a big travel group, so he is quite excited. In high spirits, Little Wang greets everyone, talking loudly while distributing white travel hats and nametags.

An hour after the scheduled departure time, the sirens finally sound. The North Korean train has arrived at long last. It is different from any other I have ever seen, still running on steam and pulling only three or four cars, the shortest train in the world. The color of the compartments is green with yellow stripes below and above the windows. This design is typical of the passenger trains running on China's major railways a few decades ago.

The locomotive chugs forward, then goes into reverse, as if the engine were being tested.

The interior looks clean. White, patterned sheer window curtains flutter in the afternoon breeze. The red velvet covers on the soft seats are eye-catching. Two glorified portraits of Kim Il Sung and his son Kim Jong Il, both in Mao jackets, are hung on the center wall. Their faces glow with a holy redness. Their determined eyes look straight ahead.

I carry my blue bag and move towards a seat near the front entrance. Before I get close, however, a man stands up abruptly. His wrinkled brown coat is worn out and dusty. His face is dark, bony with empty cheeks. It looks very cold, void of any expression. A badge, showing Kim Jong Il standing in front of a flying red flag, pinned above one of his breast pockets is the only thing colorful about him. His lips locked, he moves his hands in the air toward me as if to push me back. Obviously he does not want me to get near him.

As the train sounds a long siren, several male attendants hop on board. They all wear light gray railway uniforms and broad-rimmed hats. Their shoulders are wide, but their bodies hollow. Their faces are very lean with sunken eyes and protruding cheeks. They do not look well nourished. Nevertheless, the men appear highly capable, quick and agile in action. Their faces betray no traces of dissatisfaction. Underlying their toughness,

I see passionate loyalty and unwavering belief in their great leader Kim Jong Il.

Several clean-cut North Korean businesspeople, dragging huge boxes, climb on board. Their eyes never look at us, as if we never existed. Ordinary North Koreans are forbidden to come into the carriages, for it is a serious crime to mingle with foreigners. So they stand next to the conductor. The Chinese characters printed on the exterior of the containers tell me that they have gone to Ji'an to get food.

At around 2:30 in the afternoon Beijing time, the train begins to move, churning along at a snail's pace. Slowly, it crosses the Yalu River. When we have barely passed the borderline in the middle of the bridge, a stout train attendant jumps up from his seat and shuts all the train windows. Our Chinese guide Little Wang now stands side by side with a Korean man under the two Kims' portraits. Both of the guides are all smiles, but the message they deliver is not pleasant at all. With a microphone in hand, Little Wang translates the rules and regulations issued by the North Korean government: "Please hand over all your cell phones to our Korean comrades. Remember, you cannot call anyone at any point during the entire trip. From here, all the way to the city of Manpo, absolutely no photographs are allowed. Whoever violates these rules will not only have their equipment confiscated, but will also be detained."

Faces of the passengers are cloudy. Feeling threatened, I begin asking myself, "Is it going to be a happy trip?"

Our train chugs forward at only 15 kilometers an hour. This gives me ample time to observe the outside. Suffering from the most serious drought in three hundred years, the brown earth is cracked. It has not rained for months. The sun always rises in the morning and sets at evening, sucking away the damp soils covering the farmland and killing the young maize. This means more North Koreans here will become hungry. Some of the rivers, streams and reservoirs are almost empty. This sad scene reminds me of the dry yellow dust that engulfed the cities and farmland in Northern China. But people did not die there.

Dilapidated farmhouses and rundown workshops dot the landscape. The steep mountains stretch endlessly into the distance. North Korea is a hilly country; mountains cover most of the land. Many of them appear patched, with bald spots, because farmers and soldiers have cut down forests to cultivate more terraced fields, to use as firewood, and to trade lumber to China in exchange for corn. Without trees, the mountains can no longer hold the rainwater that will come once the drought ends, resulting in devastating floods that also ruin crops on a large scale. It is a vicious cycle.

The peasant cottages are painted grayish white, a color quite popular with the Koreans. The sheds have cracked walls and thatched roofs, or roofs with broken tiles or even without tiles at all. The houses slant seriously and seem in danger of falling at any time.

We pass one stark, poor village after another. Having focused all its attention on the Pyongyang area, the North Korean government has long neglected this mountainous mining district, which has no important cities, not even a good highway.

Scattered men, women, and children walk slowly on the hilly dirt roads. Their clothes are old and monotonous. Men wear either gray or brown uniforms. Women are usually dressed in a shabby white shirt and thin black pants. Few signs of life in the villages: no cows, no horses, and no dogs. Modern machinery does not exist here. To carry things, women put jars or white bags on their heads. Men put heavy sacks on their backs. The villagers walk draggingly with their heads low and their mouths closed, neither talking nor smiling. Children do not laugh or play. Only life-sized slogans and colorful pictures of Kim Il Sung, smiling and waving, command village entrances, where soldiers in Soviet-style army uniforms stand on guard or patrol the muddy lanes.

That afternoon around 3:30 Beijing time, 4:30 Pyongyang time, we arrive at Manpo Station. A distance of 10 kilometers from Ji'an has taken us an entire hour. As the train enters the station, the first thing that catches my attention is an enormous portrait of Kim Il Sung hung at the center of the station building. Next to the portrait is a big display board with his words on it: "Manpo is a good place. Everyone should come here for a visit."

When Kim Il Sung was alive, he did visit Manpo, one of the poorest places in the country, several times. Wherever he went in the country, people would set up monuments to celebrate the occasion. The North Koreans take his every word as scripture.

The train comes to a complete stop and passengers stand up, stretching their arms and legs. With all the windows shut to prevent us from talking to the local people or seeing anything too clearly, the air inside feels suffocating. No one would open the locked train door. Outside the windows, I see soldiers with pistols running around the oblong-shaped platform. They station themselves at our train doors, yelling and shoving away innocent passersby. Plainclothes policemen and the North Korean travel guides who will accompany us for the entire trip stand in line next to the armed soldiers, forming a human wall at each side of the empty platform.

From my seat in the train, I can see that the dim waiting room has no electric lighting. Its main door does not open to the platform, but to the side. The passengers, in order to get on board, have to go through several checkpoints and repeated inspections. People pack the waiting room and steal glances at us now and then. Their postures are stiff, their necks tight, and their faces expressionless. They stand there like stone statues. Only their elusive eyes show a glimmer of curiosity, a sign of life. I well understand their xenophobia. During the sixties and seventies, the Chinese government also prohibited ordinary Chinese from talking to foreigners. Violators were national traitors. People avoided foreigners as if they were monsters. But the mentality was conflicting. Curiously, they still wanted to see what kind of clothes the foreigners wore, what kind of equipment they carried in front of their chests, what language they spoke, and what perfume they used that smelled different. They wanted to know about the outside world, but were afraid of the punishment, which could sometimes be as harsh as the death sentence.

A train station is a smaller version of society, a realistic reflection of life. During North Korea's decade-long famine, many tragic stories have been told about its waiting rooms. Since trains no longer run on schedule, hungry people are often trapped in the station for days with nothing to eat. A typical story would go like this:

At meal time, an old lady watches a young man swallowing a piece of bread. She licks her lips then closes her mouth. After much hesitation, she approaches the young man, begging, "I haven't eaten for days. Young man, please be merciful...."

The young man stops eating. He seems ashamed. He looks at the food in his hand and does not know what to do. Finally, he replies, "You know, granny, I have sold my jacket for this piece of bread. I feel so weak and my legs are shaking. Without food, I may not be able to go home alive."

Moistening her lips again, the old woman lowers her head in silence. But her fingers are trembling obviously from hunger. She returns to her seat and sits there quietly. When the train finally comes, maybe one day, two days or three days later, the old woman can no longer stand up to catch it. If people care to look at her carefully, she may already have died some time ago.

Our train door opens suddenly. The North Korean hitchhikers standing next to the conductor get off, pulling the huge boxes of Chinese goods behind them. We also stand up, following the merchants to the door.

"Don't move. Everyone stay seated!" Out of nowhere, a middle-aged man with rough features stops us. The man's wide-shouldered frame makes him resemble a typical northern Chinese, and even his Mandarin carries a heavy northern accent. Seeing our perplexity, he explains that he learned his Chinese from a Volunteer Army soldier from Shandong Province. "Like teacher, like student," he jokes, "but I am a real Korean. I am not Chinese. I have never been to China."

The air inside the carriages becomes more and more stifling. We have already been locked here for hours. Standing below my window, a cold-looking young soldier guards the door. In despair, the confused Chinese men begin smoking, one cigarette after another. Another half an hour has passed and people are becoming impatient.

"What are we waiting for?"

No one knows.

At long last, a soldier in a short-sleeved army uniform boards the train. In front of us, he puts on a pair of white gloves.

"We will conduct a search," the Korean interpreter speaks. The soldier does not nod for greeting. Since I sit near the front door, the soldier starts with me. As ordered, I open my blue travel bag: on top are several tomatoes and cucumbers that I bought in Ji'an. The soldier takes out the vegetables and puts them aside. Then, he opens my white leather purse.

He checks everything in the purse carefully. He looks at napkins, a blank scribble pad, a ball pen, and a small bottle of prescribed medicine. The night before, I poured the pills out of the original bottle from K-Mart Pharmacy and put them into a China-made medicine bottle with Chinese characters on it. The soldier snatches the scribble pad and leafs through it. I have already torn away the pages with English words. He puts it down and opens the coin pocket of the purse. Suddenly, his eyes light up. He sees my camcorder lying at the bottom of the bag. He takes it out, turns it around and looks at it inside out.

"This is a family camcorder," I try to speak in a calm voice. He should not confiscate it. Although the North Korean government bans the professional video cameras used by journalists, officially it says that it still allows personal camcorders for home use only. However, despite the official approval, the soldier questions me and examines the equipment with suspicion.

Without my knowing it, the passengers behind me have already formed a long line in the aisle. The soldier puts down the camcorder and goes on to the next person. Slowly, I put my items back into the blue bag. My eyes continue to follow that pair of hands in white gloves busily searching through the bags and suitcases. We may have secretly regretted ever coming to such a state. But at the moment, we are already deep in the county and subject to the mercy of the North Korean government. The message being sent to us is that we all must be cooperative. This is a government that closely resembles the regime under Mao. In a way, it is even worse, because it never worries about its international reputation or any other consequences of its actions.

Outside, armed soldiers quickly fill the platform. If the search discovers any "terrorists," "international spies," "assassins," or "enemies of the state," they will have no way to escape. Other than looking for weapons, the soldier is particularly interested in notepads, letters, pamphlets, any written and printed materials containing ideological words. He is even suspicious about the plane tickets with their colorful advertisements.

Ever since China launched its reforms in the eighties, and especially after it established diplomatic relations with South Korea, North Korea has regarded its ally as a revisionist country, a traitor to communism. It openly criticizes China and has distanced itself from its giant neighbor by setting up barriers on their common border. Before, people of both sides could cross freely to each other's territory. Now, the *Workers Daily*, mouthpiece of the Korean Workers Party, calls on the North Korean people to "tuck the mosquito net tightly to prevent any capitalist cultural and ideological infiltration."

The doors finally open as the soldier orders us to get off the train. In the center of the platform, our Chinese guide Little Wang sets down the colorful plastic stools that he brought from Ji'an. We sit with our legs bent in front of our chests, waiting in this awkward position for the next train. Armed soldiers and plainclothes policemen watch us from all sides, making sure that no one wanders away from the platform center to talk with the ordinary North Korean citizens.

The soft plastic stool is shaking from under me. I hang my head low, feeling depressed. The trip has hardly begun and I am already looking forward to the end of it.

3. The Travel Guards

The wait seems forever and the small stool is by no means comfortable. Few other countries in this world treat travelers in such an insulting way. Several times I stand up, stretching my arms and legs, walking back and forth on the platform. Each time I come close to the soldiers guarding the platform, they whistle sharply and frantically gesture me back to the center.

The only people allowed to move around the platform are some workmen. Wearing typical Korean round-brimmed straw hats, they push handcarts back and forth, unloading food picked up by our train in China's Ji'an. They bow their heads, bending their upper bodies and biting their lips while hauling the heavy wooden cart.

When late afternoon approaches, the bright sun disappears suddenly. The sky becomes overcast and windy. As I put on my sweater, it pours. Rain washes the grayish, old residential buildings near the train station. Water leaks through the window-holes. Smoke-darkened chimneys made from thin sheets of iron sway in the storm. Several bare-headed teenagers rush to the center of the storm and let the rain soak them. Only hours after we enter the country, it rains at last, relieving the drought that has scorched the troubled land for months.

Water accumulates inches deep and soon floods the ground, creating many puddles, deep and shallow. In almost all the North Korean cities, the sewage systems are already out-of-date and nonfunctional. The polluted water poisons city residents, who suffer not only from hunger but also from contagious diseases such as tuberculosis and from liver cancer caused by the filthy water they drink every day.[1]

With no lights, a dark mist surrounds us, enveloping the trees, the sky, the five-storied residential buildings, the platforms. Crowds of North Korean passengers are confined in the cramped waiting room. Under the cover of heavy rain, people steal glances at us more boldly and directly.

Thunderstorms do not last long. Soon the black clouds disappear, and the sky clears up. The air after the rain smells fresh. Our train arrives. We abandon the small stools as soon as we can, and quickly settle ourselves on the comfortable train seats, hoping it will leave soon. I take the front seats reserved for the attendants, who are there to guard the door to prevent any escape. One of the Korean guides, a slim girl speaking beautiful Mandarin, sees me always alone and recommends that I sit with her countrymen.

Beside our "luxury" train is another train for North Koreans only, which looks as if it were constructed of cardboard. The windows have no glass or frames. The seats are no more than pieces of raw boards nailed together. But even this is limited, for only a few can sit; most stand. The floor is covered with dirty planks loosely placed together with wide openings in between; one can see the rails beneath. Two thin boys stick their heads out. Their heads appear disproportionately larger than their skinny bodies, which are wrapped in rags. Their knotted hair is dry and thin. Their eyes look hollow in their wide-framed faces. Their dirty noses are running; they wipe them with their sleeves from time to time. They obviously suffer from malnutrition. Still they smile sweetly at us, showing crooked, yellow teeth. Never once do they stretch out their hands to beg. Bottles of soft drink, small packages of cookies, and other refreshments are thrown from this train towards the children. On the other side, heads duck to give room.

On February 11, 2002, the United Nations World Food Program reported that about two million North Korean children are nearing death from malnutrition. In November 2002, the figure had doubled—four million.[2]

The North Korean passengers look like war refugees, their faces gaunt, their hair untrimmed, long and rumpled. But these are actually North Korea's elite. Only well-to-do people with solid political standing and good jobs can afford the expensive train tickets and obtain permission to travel, which together will cost an ordinary worker almost a month's salary if he luckily still receives it. Since fuel is scarce, few vehicles run. People walk everywhere. Foreigners may wonder if the North Koreans know that automobiles and airplanes have become an essential part of daily life elsewhere in the world. They do not look angry or complain because they have already accepted that cars have nothing to do with them. Other than a few elites in Pyongyang, everyone is the same: legs are their most reliable means of transportation.

It is hard to imagine such a primitive country existing in today's world. Japan and South Korea, both huge auto manufacturers, are only a few hundred miles away.

The six North Korean guides will "accompany" us throughout the trip. The young guides, two men and two women, are all recent graduates of the elite Pyongyang College of Foreign Languages, which is second only to the country's top Kim Il Sung University located in downtown Pyongyang. The college offers Russian, Chinese, Arabic, Japanese, and other languages. Many students also study English. The college uses the best teachers, and only native speakers are qualified to teach there.[3] During the first month of schooling, the students are forced to speak the target language in greetings until they are fluent with correct pronunciation. Upon graduation, the students, now regarded as foreign language experts, will work in important posts dealing with foreign affairs, or receive further special training to become international spies.

Our guides are well educated. None of them have been to China, but they speak fluent Mandarin Chinese. I even think they speak Chinese with a more standard pronunciation of Mandarin than I do because I grew up in Southern China and my Chinese is tinted with the local accent. One lanky young man tells me that he had started out by learning French at the Pyongyang College of Foreign Languages, but before he achieved fluency, he shifted to Chinese, since it is the most useful foreign language in North Korea.

To be a travel guide is a highly regarded job in the country, for anyone who deals with foreigners must be politically trustworthy, personally loyal to Kim Jong Il, and have a strong belief in Korean-style socialism. Traveling with foreigners, the guides eat in the best restaurants, stay in five-star hotels, and visit all the scenic spots. These positions are open only to those with powerful family backgrounds: their parents must be well connected to the Workers Party. One of the young guides, a chubby girl, has a father who is the personal secretary of Kim Jong Il.

Unlike their poor and starving countrymen, these young guides wear modern clothes and change every day. The young girls' dresses and skirts are very elegant in color and style. Even my Korean Chinese friend Suyi, who lived in South Korea for years, cannot help admiring them: "these outfits "must have been bought in Seoul."

Guide Kim is a short man in his fifties and speaks Chinese with a heavy Shanghai accent. His Chinese language teacher, a Volunteer Army soldier, is from that region. Since North Korea has always been short of men, especially after the Korean War, thousands of Chinese Volunteer soldiers were ordered to stay behind and marry the North Korean women in order to increase the population.

Guide Kim used to work at a research institute studying China before he was summoned to take this "key" job. Having studied China for his entire life, he is a true specialist.

The short, soft-spoken man can recite hundreds of ancient T'ang poems:

> My old friend flew away on a flying crane,
> And left empty the Crane Pavilion....

He loves Chinese revolutionary songs such as "Socialism is really Great!" and "Americans are the Ambitious Wolves." He sings these throughout the trip.

Despite his seniority and decades of working experience, his salary is only 130 Korean won ($65), the same as the young college graduates. He says, "Our society is a classless society. Everyone is equal. It doesn't matter if you are old or young, man or woman. We all receive the same pay. I am satisfied with what I have. Money doesn't have much use to me. Tell you the truth, I don't know how to use my salary since our government takes care of everything."

Guide Kim's family of six live in a two-bedroom apartment on a major avenue in Pyongyang. Once a couple gets married, the government will assign them a place to live at no cost. Guide Kim does not pay utilities, not even the water bill. Medical treatment is free for everyone. And the eleven-year education is free and mandatory. The country has eliminated illiteracy. The state also pays college education if the high school graduate can get accepted. The North Koreans are the most educated population in the world: about 30 percent of the adults are college graduates.

"We North Koreans enjoy the best benefits that a socialist system can offer. Even movies are free. Can you believe that?" Guide Kim smiles. He is very proud of his country.

"I know in Northeast China, unemployed workers are everywhere, wandering on the streets to look for opportunities. With no stable income, they wage strikes to protest. Everyday, countless people in China are losing their jobs because of the capitalist economy, because machines have replaced people. But we don't have any unemployment problems here. Everyone's job is guaranteed. Look, while everyone in China cares about how to make money, what I am worrying most about is how to serve people well. To be specific, I must serve you well, our comrades, this is my job, so when you go back to China, you will tell others that the North Koreans are the happiest people in the world thanks to our great leader Kim Il Sung and our dear leader Kim Jong Il." The defected party secretary Hwang Jang Yop once angrily says, about his countryman, "Can we call people sane when they talk of having built an utopia for the workers and peasants when the workers and peasants are starving?"

"Do Pyongyang residents still receive rations?" a passenger asks. Guide Kim's face loses some of its brightness, but he tries to paint a rosy picture of his nation. However, his pale face tells it all. He once says that it takes him only three minutes to finish a meal because there is really not much on the dinner table to eat. Later he changes his story and says that he has a stomach problem and cannot bear too much food. I begin wondering Guide Kim's sanity.

Besides natural disasters of drought and flood, one of the major causes of North Korea's current famine lies in the government's centrally planned economic policies. The Korean Workers Party decides when to grow crops, when to separate seedlings, when to harvest, and how to harvest. The Workers Party is also in charge of such details as to how to process and store food and how much of food crops a farmer can receive.[4] The Workers Party takes all the initiative away from the farmers, who do not care if the Party misses the growing season or grows on the wrong season. They farm without motivation, without incentives.

In North Korea, prices, interest rates, and exchange rates have nothing to do with the market. The economic policies ignore the rules of supply and demand, favoring political incentives instead of material rewards to motivate people. The government develops heavy and military industries at the expense of light and consumer ones. Nonproductive activities such as the construction of large-scale monuments and exhibition halls for the great leaders have also consumed large revenues and labor.

Today's North Korea is short of almost everything: salt, sugar, cooking oil, cotton, paper, electronics, energy, textiles, and transportation. Even in Pyongyang, the city that enjoys the best and steadiest food supplies, every resident can receive only 12 kilograms of grain, 30 grams of oil, 20 grams of soybean sauce, 20 grams of salt, a tiny piece of meat and a few eggs every month. When times are bad, the grain ration could be cut to five kilograms.[5] Although the meager monthly supply of all but grain for a Pyongyang resident is not enough for an American family to consume in a day, the thing he feels lucky for is that he still receives food regularly. For people in other cities, such a stable food supply is not guaranteed.

For this the North Koreans blame Mother Nature and America. Guide Kim cannot hide his indignation. "The United States is our dead enemy.

We hate them. If not for them, we wouldn't have to spend so heavily on building a big army, we wouldn't have to make nuclear weapons for self-defense. We could have used the money for our socialist construction. All because of their economic sanctions, we have no gasoline, no buses; we have no money to buy tires and food. Our people suffer so much all because of the United States. Since it treats us as its enemy, we treat it the same. We will never yield even if it means that we will have difficulties for a long time; we will never bow even if we are the last socialist country in the world. Our government is ready for war, and everyone in the country is ready. Everyone is a soldier when fighting breaks out, and we will fight to the end."

Guide Kim's voice is thin but his emotion is strong, representative of the anti-American sentiment of North Koreans. On the streets of cities huge propaganda poster boards call for war:

"We are already prepared!"

"We are ready. Are you ready?"

"I am ready every minute."

"We are all the successors of communism. We are the masters of our future."

"But the United States has provided the most food aid to North Korea," I lose my vigilance one time and blurt out.

"Nonsense!" Guide Kim retorts instantly, "The Americans offered three billion dollars to obtain permission to inspect our nuclear reactor sites. When we agreed, they changed their minds. Instead of paying money, they decide to give us food. What is good about them? There is no human side. All is business."

Guide Kim is so offended that he bans me from using my camcorder for almost half a day. He changes his attitude only after I offer him a hat to express my friendliness.

Guide Kim and his comrades are not just travel guides. They are also propaganda tools, taking every opportunity to praise the Kims and promote Juche, the country's political religion. Meanwhile, they are also plain-clothes policemen, watching closely our every move.

So are the young train attendants. Highly vigilant, they treat every foreigner as a possible spy and an enemy. They monitor us to make sure that we do nothing to sabotage the regime during our short visit to the country. The guides, the train attendants, and later the cameramen have all formed a powerful alliance against us. I have never felt so restricted psychologically and physically.

4. En Route to Mt. Myohyang

Slowly, our train rumbles towards Mt. Myohyang, a famous scenic spot about 105 kilometers from the city of Manpo. An attendant in his thirties takes a seat opposite mine. A typical Korean man, he is of a robust build. His face is dark, and his slim eyes look even slimmer under his bushy eyebrows. The gray uniform looks sizes bigger than his bony frame.

He smiles at me. That is unusual. My impression of the Korean men is that they never smile.

"Do you like the train?" he speaks in broken Chinese, pointing to the windows covered with sheer curtains.

"Very much!" I try to be polite, although the train is just normal even according to Chinese standards.

"It is the best train in our country," his voice is full of satisfaction. "Just for people like you," he emphasizes while looking around in appreciation.

Conversation in Chinese is difficult for him. He uses gestures, trying to make himself understood. He grabs a pen and writes down Chinese characters. Most Koreans, whether from the North or South, understand written Chinese. But the North Korean government, insisting on national superiority, dignity, and independence, refused to teach it in schools. Only recently, the ban has been lifted, following the lead of South Korea. "If they study Chinese, we should, too. Why don't we do it?" Guide Kim tells us.

The train attendant is a college graduate who majored in engineering. Most factories in the country have shut down either because of energy shortages or because the workers all left to look for food. With only a few plants still operating, and even those at only 25 to 30 percent of their original capacity,[1] a train attendant is the best career for the man's college degree. No matter what, the job has something to do with a train, which means modern technology in North Korea. Thirty-three, he is already married with two children. He has a good family background: both his parents are working proletariats. That is why his family is allowed to live in Pyongyang. His eyes glistening with tears, he says that he misses home very much. He has a younger brother whom he also loves dearly. The conversation goes on as we struggle with gestures. Suddenly he utters in English, "Can you speak English?"

"Sure I can."

"My English is better than my Chinese. I like English and study it during my spare time."

I am surprised that the North Koreans are allowed to learn and speak the language that the Americans speak. During China's Cultural Revolution, those who studied English secretly were labeled "running dogs of the American imperialists" if they were discovered.

"Do school children learn English?" I ask.

"Yes, they learn English in primary schools, but for only a few years."

"Do you like your job?"

He nods.

"Do you have enough to eat?" Looking at his pointed face, I cannot keep from asking. Inquiry about if one has enough to eat or not is a natural way to show concern in the Orient.

He pretends that he does not understand me, looking at me with a blank face.

"Is your life OK?"

He bites his lips and looks outside the window.

It is dinner time.

The dining car is spacious and the tables are shining clean. Portraits of Kim Il Sung and Kim Jong Il tremble with the movement of the train.

The elder Kim's words hang on the front wall: "What is most important in the ideological revolution is to arm the Party members and working people with our Party's revolutionary idea, the Juche idea."[2]

Food is already on the table. The young Korean women in striped uniforms are eager to serve. Their faces are full and smooth, the skin fair and fine; their lips are full and naturally red; their hair is dark and thick, still in the traditional style. The North Korean government knows the value of its unpolluted women and uses them like flowers to decorate the country, planting them on the important streets in Pyongyang and other showy places to impress foreign visitors. The North Korean women have traditionally been nice to Chinese men, whom they always link with the Volunteer Army soldiers who crossed Yalu River to save their country during the Korean War.

Before dinner, Guide Kim declares loudly, "It is Korean women's greatest pleasure to serve you Chinese men. We will remember your kindness generation after generation."

Next to my table, a young waitress unfolds a napkin and places it on a Chinese man's lap. She arranges the stainless steel spoon and chopsticks to the best angle for him to use and pours beer into the cup in front of him. The only thing that she does not do, I think, is to feed him personally.

The first dinner for us is quite rich. Korean rice, considered the best in the world, is creamy and glistening, sending out fresh fragrance. The meat, however, is not well cooked; baked chicken legs, regarded the best part for a chicken in East Asia, taste dry and without flavor. All the other small plates, about a dozen or so, contain various Korean hot pickles. For the Chinese guests, whose lives have seen fundamental changes during the decades of economic reforms, the food is too rough to swallow even if the dishes are the best the North Koreans can provide. There are a lot of leftovers on each table; the waitresses carefully put them aside.

From my seat at the first row, I can see the kitchen clearly. It is not well equipped. No dishwashers, no sanitary equipment at all, not even refrigerators. A man is washing bowls and plates in cold water. He dries them with a towel and then takes them out to serve the next group of diners. When the man finds out that I am watching him, he quietly draws the curtain to block my view.

After our dinner, the guides and train attendants form a line in the aisle, awaiting their turn. They walk like army soldiers to the dining car and shut the door closely behind them.

"What do they eat? Why do they have to shut the door?"

Out of curiosity, I stand up and go to the dining car. Inside, six people surround a table for four, bowing their heads over the bowls and devouring silently.

"What do you want?" A man who looks like the chef asks me with his mouth still chewing. His voice is thick and rude.

"I am very thirsty and want some water."

He points to the table near the door, where a thermos bottle and a pile of teacups are located. I fill one with hot water. The dining car suddenly turns deadly quiet. I raise my head: everyone has stopped eating and is watching me with hostility. Their angry eyes force me to turn back. The moment I walk out, someone slams the door behind me.

In about half an hour, the North Koreans come back in twos and threes. The train attendants take their seats near me. Faint red clouds color rises on their lean faces. They quietly smack their lips. On the small train tables, a Korean waitress has placed several raw peaches, hard and tiny as walnuts. The green fruits are still too young to be harvested. The attendants, still hungry after dinner, use their sleeves to clean the peaches and begin chewing resonantly.

The train squeaks along slowly. It is the strangest ride I have ever taken. Our isolated special "express" connects and disconnects with cargo wagons along the way. It runs ahead for a while, then stops and reverses. The trip has cured insomnia in most of the passengers. Those that remain awake play cards to while away time. The girl attendant begins reading. Her book is made from repeatedly recycled paper: it is grayish, very coarse with many pimples. The words are unclear, so her eyes squint at times. A man in army uniform riding on horseback stands out on the crimson book cover. A huge flag with a sickle and hammer, the Party flag, is flying in the background. Needless to say, it is another book worshipping Kim Il Sung and Kim Jong Il, which is the sole purpose for the literary arts and publishing industry in North Korea.

Then, for no apparent reason, the train suddenly grinds to a halt. I walk to the door and pop my head out to take fresh air. Whispers are coming from underneath the train. Maintenance workers crawling on the rails are knocking here and there with small hammers for inspection. The gentle breeze blows in but does not carry the familiar songs of insects in summer nights. On the famished land, even they seem too hungry to sing. From the platform emerge several shadows, each holding a flashlight and a tiny hammer. Startled to see me, they murmur, quickly walking away in line.

After my eyes get adjusted to the darkness outside, I can distinguish the outlines of the houses beside the railway. Only a few faint beams flicker from the "windows." People are afraid of turning on their lights because they attract robbers. In times this bad, lights in the night signal warmth and wealth. Bandits, who are often starving armed soldiers, storm villages and small towns as soon as dusk falls. They believe that these people, if they can afford to burn lights during the night, must have food and money. Most likely, these people have Chinese relatives who keep on sending them assistance.

During the daytime, the notorious soldier robbers, carrying clubs and rocks, wait at the roads. They stop vehicles and strip passengers of clothes, food, and money. They beat to death anyone who resists. The government does nothing to stop them. If it cannot satisfy the Army, let it help itself.[3]

Below the train, the intermittent knocking still goes on. With all win-

The empty Mt. Myohyang train station. The North Korean people have all been driven away because of us. Plain-clothes policemen patrol the deserted platform.

dows closed, the carriages are hot. Some of the passengers stop playing cards and look into the dark night, wondering. The night seems endless, and the ride is torturing indeed.

After nearly an hour and a half, the knocking finally recedes. A railway guard waves a small flag in the darkness. The train takes off again, running in its haphazard fashion.

At eleven o'clock at night, we arrive at the Myohyang station. It takes about 7 hours to cover 105 kilometers. On the empty platform, the one or two yellow lights waver like the eyes of ghosts. This time, no armed soldiers crowd to round us up. There is no need for it since no ordinary North Korean people are allowed to travel at this hour. Inside the train station, only the Duty Office is dimly lit. Through the open windows, I see railway workers sitting around a table under the faint lights inches above their Soviet-style caps. Three large Japanese-made shuttle buses already wait at the platform.

Guide Kim and the chubby North Korean girl are assigned to our Bus Number 2. The girl never smiles or speaks to us. In fact, she never really says anything, but sits quietly with Little Wang at the back of the bus. Her job is to watch us from behind while Guide Kim supervises us at the front. The girl never hides her fondness of Little Wang. In front of everyone, she puts her arms around the young man's neck. Nor is she shy about sharing the hotel room with him. Unlike China, the North Korean government seems quite open-minded about relationships between the sexes. Men and women can hold hands and show their intimacy in public. Behaviors like this were strictly forbidden for Chinese youth before the economic reforms in the eighties.

On a piece of flat land in the valleys of Mt. Myohyang stands the Hyangsan Hotel. North Korea does not have enough good hotels to accommodate travelers in great numbers. This is one of the few that reluctantly meet world standards. Seen from afar, the construction resembles a big diamond shedding numerous beams of light. The design is novel, with vaulted ceilings and grayish marble throughout the interior. A fountain adorns the grand lobby, with a statuary deer drinking by the creek against a cliff.

The hotel is built more to impress than to serve. Its check-in area is so huge that it can hold hundreds of people at one time, though it has never reached that capacity. Chinese merchandise, mainly fast food, and Korean paintings and art crafts are on display in the small shops located on both sides of the lobby. Propaganda posters on the main wall near the elevator portray the smiling Kim Il Sung inspecting schools equipped with XT computers. Surrounded by the happy children, the Great Leader carries a little girl in his arms. Below the picture are Kim's words, "Education is decisive for the revolution and the fate of the nation. Without education there can be neither social progress nor national prosperity...."

The splendid hotel mainly serves Chinese tourists, international diplomats, and high-ranking officials of the Korean Workers Party, as well as many North Korean university students who were born or grew up in Japan. These expatriates can board a ferry from Japan to North Korea to take a week-long trip, savoring their fatherland's glorious mountains and rivers, and worshipping Kim Il Sung and Kim Jong Il. No ordinary North Koreans can enter the Hyangsan Hotel.

My room is on the third floor. It has two single beds, a bedside table in between and a TV in front. The striped sheets are spread casually over the mattresses, not tucked in like in all the other hotels of this class in the world. The cotton blanket is put in a cover, which has a diamond-shaped opening in the middle to expose the red color. The pillows are filled with husks; they are believed to cool the head during the hot summer months. The phone is still rotary — touch-tone has not come here — and one cannot dial long distance. The bathroom is modern with smooth tiles, but the gray-yellow color looks dull.

The central air conditioning makes small buzzing noises from time

The diamond-shaped Hyangsan Hotel in the Mt. Myohyang resort area was also built to impress the foreigners.

to time. Since electricity is extremely scarce, the hotel has carefully adjusted it to the most power-saving temperature. I turn on the TV, but the screen is blank.

The next morning, I awake to the pleasant hymn of the chirping birds and the peaceful sound of the waterfalls from Mt. Myohyang. Standing on the balcony, I savor the scenery. A Korean man in white is sweeping the road, using a big broom made from reeds. He bends his body so low that his face almost touches the ground. He picks up the slightest paper shreds, cigarette butts and other items.

It is a fresh morning. Embraced by the lavish mountains, this majestic hotel seems like a castle in a paradise. It is hard for me to imagine that a horrible human tragedy is unfolding behind the beauty, quietly taking lives by the thousands and millions.

On the mountain road, pedestrians carrying white cloth bags walk with small but hurried steps. They hang their heads low, their eyes glued to the stone steps underneath their feet. School children in white and blue uniforms with red scarves around their necks soon join them. Those in primary school carry backpacks, while older children hold Soviet-style handbags, which resemble a briefcase. A tall boy sees something by the roadside and bends down quickly to pick it up, carefully putting it in his bag. I have noticed that almost everyone, student or not, carries some kind of bag with them. They put into it anything that might be useful: a grain of rice, edible wild vegetables, twigs, a piece of paper, wires, wood scraps, nuts and whatnot.[4]

Military trucks drive past once in a while with a full load of armed soldiers. Besides these vehicles, I see no public buses, cargo trucks, delivery vans, school buses, or any means of transportation for civilian use during this morning rush hour.

Our breakfast is rice soup with a small piece of steamed bread and two thin slices of butter for each person. Also served are a variety of pickles, known as kimchee, in numerous plates. The Koreans make these pickles from cabbages preserved in salt and red pepper powder. Traditionally, every Korean eats kimchee every day for every meal. But now kimchee has become a luxury and has long since disappeared from normal people's dinner tables.

The waitresses, dressed in hanboks, traditional robes of red, green, yellow, and orange, flit back and forth like butterflies. Men stand up frequently to take pictures with them. Stirring songs from the loudspeakers resound throughout the vast banquet hall, praising Kim Il Sung and Kim Jong Il:

> Our great leader!
> You are the sun of 21st Century.
> You are like mother to me!
> Without veins, a melon will die.
> Without mother, a child will suffer.
> We are the sunflowers that forever turn to the sunlight.
> The rocks in the Diamond Mountain are strong,
> But not as strong as our will to follow you.
> We will charge when you give the order.
> We will shed every drop of our blood to protect you.

5. Kim Il Sung, God in North Korea

As if three guides on one bus were still not enough, a fourth person, a cameraman, joins us. A plump young man, he wears a fashionable shirt with yellow stripes. Carrying a Sony video camera, he follows us closely. His filming will be aired on TV as part of a government propaganda campaign aiming to show the North Korean people how popular their country is since so many foreigners come to admire it.

We start out early in the morning. Our bus makes a few turns on the mountain road. Before long, it stops in front of a magnificent temple with a light green façade of glazed tiles and pink flying roof. Built in a valley against a hill of lush pine trees and huge cypresses, the temple blends well with the natural surroundings. This must have been the best location that Kim Il Sung could find when he built his International Friendship Exhibition Hall in the seventies.

Standing motionless like statues, honorary guards in white gloves protect the heavy gates. Young women in traditional gowns greet us with sweet smiles. Their colorful dresses are dazzling. The green mountains, the shining temple, and the beautiful women and handsome men make me believe for a moment that I have arrived in a fairyland.

Suyi, the plump Korean-Chinese woman in our tourist group, knows how these young Koreans come here. "Don't be deceived by their uniform and beautiful dresses. The young people are actually personal servants of Kim Il Sung and Kim Jong Il. It is a public secret that they work as honor guards, hostesses, security, or private nurses in the Parliamentary Hall on

Kim Il Sung's heavily guarded, splendid Internationl Friendship Exhibition Hall at Mt. Myohyang. One of his numerous villas and palaces is also hidden away in the mountain.

Mt. Kumsu, International Friendship Exhibition Halls here in Mt. Myohyang, as well as other villas of the great leaders across the country. Some of the young people do nothing but sweep the gardens throughout their ten-year service."

The job is excellent for young North Koreans because it offers a short-cut for them to climb up the social ladder. In order to be selected from hundreds of thousands of applicants, the youth must be highly intelligent, likable, and physically fit. They must go through strict physical examinations every three months and receive political checkups. Once selected, these young men and women have to cut all family contacts. During their decade-long service, only party officials can visit and speak with their families and deliver personal messages. As compensation, the families receive rare commodities such as color television sets, refrigerators and washing machines, as well as gifts from the great leaders. On New Year's Day and the birthdays of Kim Il Sung and Kim Jong Il, the families receive fruits, fish and canned food, and sometimes pictures of the great leaders. The families keep the photos as treasures for future generations to admire.

These young servants live under strict surveillance and have to keep secret what they know throughout their lives. Every minute, they risk being sent to the concentration camps because of a mistake or slip of the tongue. At the end of their ten-year service, if they haven't committed any major offenses, they are sent to study in the College of Communism, which trains ranking party officials, or enter prestigious institutes such as Kim Il Sung University. For discharged young women the Party arranges marriages with promising young men.[1]

After a short wait in front of the temple, we are met by a woman in a sky-blue gown. Whenever she mentions Kim Il Sung, her words become pronounced and devout. Tears fill her narrow eyes under her dark eyebrows.

"There are two complexes not far from each other. One is for our great leader Kim Il Sung and the other is for the dear leader Kim Jong Il. The buildings altogether occupy 360 hectares and consist of 200 display rooms, 150 for our great leader Kim Il Sung and 50 for our dear leader Kim Jong Il. During the past five decades, our great leaders have received altogether 214,600 gifts from influential people and leaders from other countries."

The woman becomes emotional: "Our great leaders don't take these valuables as their own, but display them in public for the people to see and learn. How great their selfless spirit and how noble their personal characters! How many leaders in this world like ours care about people more than themselves?"

Kim Il Sung was the founding father of North Korea. He established the Korean Workers Party and the Korean People's Army, which grew out of his guerrilla force in the Changbai Mountains (Mt. Paektu) of China during the thirties. Kim started his personality cult as early as 1949, when those who fought with the Chinese Communists came back to Korea and threatened his power. Kim began purging his personal enemies, successfully ousting the Chinese faction first, then eliminating those from the South Korean Workers Party, and later those belonging to the Soviet faction.

The core of Kim Il Sung's ideology is called "Juche," a revolutionary nationalism quite different from Marxism. In Kim's own words, Juche is a quasi-mystical concept exemplified by a supreme leader. It emphasizes the superiority of the collective over the individual and an ability to act independently without regard to outside interference.[2] Juche is not a new idea, but a version of Mao's destructive theory of self-reliance that justified his own closed-door policy, which ruled China for nearly thirty years, leading the country into one disaster after another. However, the North

Korean government enthusiastically claims that Juche is a creative application of Marxism-Leninism. In North Korea, the theory has already become equivalent to a state religion through the propaganda of mass media, and through workers' and neighborhood associations.

For fifty years, under the guiding light of this ideology, North Korea withdrew from the world, and became one of the most isolated nations on earth.

Our female hostess in the sky-blue gown hands a pair of white gloves to a tall traveler and asks him to open one of the heavy gates. The Friendship Exhibition Hall has four giant copper gates, each weighing four tons. The man uses both his hands, holding his breath, but he cannot move the door a bit. Only with the help of several other men does he eventually pull it open.

Portraits of Kim Il Sung hang in every household (North Korean government).

"This is our national treasure," the woman says, smiling broadly. "We designed and built these halls all by ourselves— this is called self-reliance, our great Juche idea. As you can see, the temple is unique. Looking from the outside, it seems to have been built of only wood, but in reality, not even an inch of wood is used. All materials are cement and steel, so it would last forever. There is another feature. Have you all seen windows?"

Yes, I see rows of windows shining in the sunlight like colorful diamonds.

"They are not real windows. They are just decorative ones. You cannot see any windows once inside. The entire building is sealed."

The interior of the building is state-of-the-art, with thick marble columns, elegant wallpaper, and plush red carpets. The light fixtures are sumptuous and sophisticated in design, emitting soft, luminous rays in every corner. The marble floor reflects our shadows, and the entire building is equipped with central air conditioning.

No photos are allowed. Those wearing hats must take them off. Guide Kim orders us to put on shoe covers and warns us not to talk to each other, for this is a sacred place.

With Guide Kim in the lead, we walk in a single line along the long corridor. The chubby girl-guide guards us, making sure we do not breach security. The corridor seems like a deep cave with many twists and turns. In the labyrinth, one can easily get lost. Wherever we go, we see ample lights. But as soon as we leave, the lights go out behind us.

Walls slide open, and suddenly I find myself in one huge room after another with countless trophies displayed in the glass cases. Three portraits hang in every display room: of Great Leader Kim Il Sung, Dear Leader Kim Jong Il, and Kim Jong Soo, the Great Mother and First Lady. Because of the sheer size of the International Friendship Exhibition Hall, it is impossible to visit every one of the 150 exhibition rooms; we see only the most important.

When we reach the Russian Room, the electricity suddenly goes off. I happen to be standing alone in the middle of the darkness. Scary voices coming from all sides make me even more nervous. I scramble to get close to the rest of the group. In darkness, one minute passes like a year. Without windows, Kim Il Sung's Friendship Hall is now a real underground tomb.

"Please stand still! Don't move," Guide Kim shouts, "Everything will be fine."

Nervous voices die down. Guide Kim says that the power outage is totally accidental and has never happened before. But from the way he handles the situation, it does not seem like his first time. North Korea suffers from a chronic energy crisis, and most areas have undependable power. There are no street lights in the evening. The power shortage is so serious that even Oun Joung-ni, Kim Jong Il's model people's commune, a showcase to the world, is dark at night with only candles wavering in a window.[3]

When power finally returns, I follow the group closely and refuse to drift far from it for even a second. The China Room is the biggest of all, full of displays given by the senior leaders of the Chinese Communist Party. The late Mao Zedong, Liu Shaoqi, and other top Chinese leaders never forgot to give Kim Il Sung gifts on every occasion: his birthday, North Korea's National Day, or the anniversary of the founding of the Workers Party. The gifts are imposing Chinese paintings of mountains and rivers, Suzhou silk embroideries, full-size lapis lazuli vases, lacquer trays, and bamboo furniture.

"We Korean people will always treasure our relationship with China. May the friendship go on and on, like the evergreen pines on Diamond Mountain," Guide Kim says with emotion, pointing to a huge vase decorated with golden roses.

At the end of the corridor we enter a splendid hall. On a wall-sized screen, brilliant beams radiate from a background of blooming pink azaleas, turning them crystal. Standing in the center is a larger-than-life wax figure of Kim Il Sung wearing dark-framed glasses and a powerful-looking Mao suit. He smiles broadly, his face glowing with health. His huge frame towers above the tourists. He is not on earth, but in heaven. This image is not a human being, but a divine figure, a god.

"Please pay respects to our Great Leader Kim Il Sung by bowing three times," Guide Kim orders. The high-pitched national anthem resounds throughout the hall, and Guide Kim's eyes turn moist.

I hate to bow to Kim. But inside the gorgeous Friendship Hall, armed soldiers hide everywhere. They are also concealed behind the compound and among the thick trees by the roads; I saw their shadows when our bus first entered the compound. Kim Il Sung's sacred Hall is a most heavily guarded place and serves as a symbol of the existing regime and Juche ideology. As Guide Kim had warned, he does not allow even the slightest expression of contempt or impoliteness in front of the great leader.

I bow three times.

"Our Great Leader President Kim Il Sung is the sun in our hearts! The sun of the 21st century! He loves us as a dear father. Our great leader is with us forever!" Guide Kim and the chubby girl-guide shout in one voice as we retreat from the Hall.

Today, the North Koreans revere Kim Il Sung more than the Chinese worshipped Mao Zedong during the mad years of the Great Cultural Revolution. Like Mao, Kim Il Sung ruled his people with an iron fist. While Mao mainly labeled people as "friends" and "enemies," Kim Il Sung, during the fifties, divided society into three main classes: "core" (28 percent), "wavering" (45 percent), and "hostile" (27 percent), based on personal loyalty to him. He set up Citizen Registration Groups to analyze people according to their social and family origins and their behaviors on eight separate occasions following the Korean War. Based on this personal information, everyone received a security rating. These ratings determined everyone's employment, higher education, residence, and medical treatment.[4]

Kim Il Sung labeled people who had relatives in South Korea the "hostile class." Those with Chinese relatives also lost their more loyal ratings after China adopted economic reforms and established diplomatic relations with South Korea in the eighties. The great leader also barred children of religious parents from receiving higher education and health care.

Even after the death of Kim Il Sung, the North Korean people still call him "The Fatherly leader of lofty benevolence and immense solicitude," "The great sun, a great man," "The Great Son of the nation, the

Great Son of the people." One newspaper article even says that "Thanks
to this great heart, national independence is firmly guaranteed."

Radio broadcasts claim, "Kim Il Sung's heart is a traction power
attracting the hearts of all people and a centripetal force uniting them as
one. No age, no person has ever seen such a great man with such a warm
love."[5]

Kim Il Sung was very confident about his good health. Just a week
before his death, he said with a laugh that he was prepared to live for
another ten years. But on July 8, 1994, he died suddenly of a heart attack
at his mansion in Mt. Myohyang. It was rumored that the great leader
fainted after having a furious quarrel with his son, Kim Jong Il, about the
famine, which had gone from bad to worse and already starved millions
to death. Vehicles could not reach him in time because no good roads lead
to his resort in the mountain.

Guide Kim says that, upon hearing news of Kim Il Sung's death, millions of people poured into Pyongyang to pay their last respects. Some
pounded their chests, knocking their heads on the ground. Some cried
uncontrollably, cursing the earth. Some even passed out with grief. Women
refused to eat for days, mourning deeply on Kim Il Sung Square. Workers
were too sad to work. Lives actually stopped.

For days and weeks, the government issued messages of condolence
that echoed everywhere in the country:

> The Central Committee of the Workers Party reports to the entire
> people of the country with the deepest grief that the great leader Com-
> rade Kim Il Sung, passed away from a sudden attack of illness at 0.2.00
> on July 8, 1994. Our respected fatherly leader who has devoted his
> whole life to the popular masses' cause of independence and engaged
> himself in tireless activities for the prosperity of the motherland and
> happiness of the people, for the reunification of our country and inde-
> pendence of the world until the last moments of his life, departed
> from us to our greatest sorrows.

Throughout the entire trip, I have kept worrying about Guide Kim
and his colleagues. Whenever they mention the two Kims, they must prop-
erly address Kim Il Sung as "our Great Leader President Kim Il Sung," and
his son "our Dear Leader Chairman Kim Jong Il." What if they accidentally say the wrong thing? The Chinese travelers pretend to look respectful, but they laugh secretly about the frenzied personal cult of the two
Kims. China's tragic past is repeating itself in today's North Korea. Why
does mankind not learn the valuable lessons achieved at the cost of life
and blood?

Kim Il Sung's signature when he visited Panmunjom on July 7, 1994. He died of a heart attack only one day later in his secluded villa at Mt. Myohyang. This monument in the DMZ was erected to inspire the North Korean military to fight to the end.

Located on the first floor of the brightly lit Friendship Hall is a small gift shop. Hung on the wall are paintings of half-naked Korean women bathing in a creek, as well as flowers and trees of all kinds. Handicrafts and small souvenirs adorn the counters. I want to buy a badge of either the younger or older Kim. Every North Korean wears it, from our guides to the army soldiers, from school children to the farmers in the fields. It has become a part of people's daily outfit, whether a military uniform or a plain-colored shirt. Even the Chinese media admits that a greater percentage of North Koreans wear badges today than the Chinese did at the peak of the Cultural Revolution.

But here, in the gift shop, the Kims' portraits and badges are nowhere to be seen.

"Do you have a badge for sale like the one you are wearing?" I ask the woman shop assistant, pointing to the one on her chest.

Her face flushing, she angrily slaps my hand back. She uses such strength that my finger knuckles make cracking sounds. Shocked, I retreat. What's wrong?

"No! Our Great Leader's badge is not for sale!" She retorts, "How could you point your finger at our Great Leader?"

If I were a North Korean, I would have been detained at once.

Guide Kim blames me for being disrespectful. He explains that the Kims' badges cannot be sold for profit. Making money on the badges is considered a big insult to the leaders. In order to get a badge for replacement if one loses it, people have to submit a written application a week in advance, explaining the reasons why they need a new badge and writing self-criticisms for not being respectful enough to the great leaders.

There is another rule that every North Korean must follow: no one can take pictures of the Kims from an angle or from the sides, or take just part of the bodies. The photographs of the great leaders must be whole and from the front. Violators are absolutely "counterrevolutionaries."

In North Korea no one can sit on newspapers bearing pictures of the Kims. Anyone who defaces a newspaper photo becomes a political criminal. If children do it accidentally, then their parents must face the consequences. Each household must hang the Kims' pictures, keep them clean and bow to them at the end of the day. Local party officials will inspect the homes unannounced once a month, and if the family is found to have neglected the photos, it will have to write self-criticisms throughout the year.[6]

Guide Kim opens a huge guest book and asks the tourists to write praises of Kim Il Sung and his grand Friendship Hall. I take a seat near a coffee table, massaging my sore knuckles.

6. *Kim Jong Il Behind the Veil*

Only fifty meters from Kim Il Sung's building lies the Friendship Hall of his son. This palace also has a pink flying roof and green glazed walls. Female hostesses with shoulder-length wavy hair stand in line, bowing and smiling. Colorful traditional dresses cover their bodies from neck to feet, hiding their contours perfectly. Their flawless complexions are smooth and clear as jade. Their voices sound deep and nasal, but resonate like metal when they mention the names of their great leaders.

The two halls for Kim Il Sung and Kim Jong Il are designed exactly the same, made from concrete and steel, and all with decorated windows. The only difference lies in their sizes. Kim Il Sung's palace contains four heavy copper gates, with each door weighing four tons, while the younger Kim has two copper gates, each weighing four-and-a-half tons.

On display here are China-made Lianxiang brand computers and laser printers sent by Chinese President Jiang Zemin, silver wine cups from Russian President Vladimir Putin, and luxurious gilded furniture from South Korean businessmen. South Korea's President Kim Dae-jung, following the summit conference in June 2002, gave Kim Jong Il a wide-screen Samsung television set and a Hyundai sedan. A CNN-logo paperweight from Ted Turner is also on display.

Oil paintings of Dutch pastures, ancient cathedrals, icy lakes and rivers, and snow-capped mountains sent by European leaders decorate the long corridor walls. The heaviest piece of ivory in the world, at 12 tons, is housed in these rooms. It is a gift from an African president.

Kim Jong Il is the General Secretary of the Korean Workers Party and Chairman of the National Defense Commission. The top leader is of medium size and always wears a green trench coat and oversized glasses. His hair is thin and receding around the forehead and above the ears. He seldom smiles and always maintains a serious look. He prefers to keep a low profile, and as a result still remains a mysterious figure to the world at large. Only in recent years has he come out somewhat from behind the concealing veil of secrecy.

Kim Jong Il, born at a Soviet military camp near Khabarovsk in 1942, is Kim Il Sung's son by his first marriage. His mother, Kim Jong-suk, was a guerrilla soldier and died in the forties. To create a mystic air, the government claims that when Kim Jong Il was born on the slopes of Paektu-san, a rainbow appears on the sky while a beautiful bird is singing praises on the future Dear Leader.

Although his country remains primitive, Kim Jong Il is a modern man. He enjoys the Internet and worships Michael Jordan and the NBA. He has a good memory and passionately loves history. Before he turned twenty, he had already read many important military tactics books.

As a small boy, Kim showed ambition. Hwang Jang-yop, a former Korean Workers Party secretary, remembers that when Kim was a little boy and played with his friends, he would like to name himself "premier" and appoint his pals "ministers." Hwang, now an old man of over seventy, watched the young Kim grow up and taught him at the prestigious Kim Il Sung University in Pyongyang. The teacher and his student finally split over Kim's plans for military expansion into South Korea. Hwang thought that Kim was insane in attempting to turn the South into "a sea of flames" and gradually lost Kim's trust. In 1997, during a conference abroad, Hwang walked out of the North Korean embassy in Beijing and defected to the South.

Kim Il Sung and Kim Jong Il differ in personality. The elder Kim was said to be mindful of advice from others, while the younger Kim is arrogant and self-centered in making decisions. The latter has a violent temper and frequently screams at staff. Suspicious and emotional, Kim openly expresses his likes and dislikes. He cannot take criticism and swiftly punishes. Unlike his father, he likes to take care of everything, from deciding which floor and room he should use for his party secretary meeting to the sort of gifts he will give. He has created a system that requires the local government agencies from all over the country to report every major daily event to the central government.

In Hwang Jang-yop's words, "Kim possesses vigorous energy, as well as unswerving will to protect his own interest. His political and artistic sense is very sharp, and his brain functions fast. Worshipped madly by the people since his birth, he has never experienced hardships. No one can make a direct telephone call to him, no matter how high his or her position is. He considers the party and military as his own and does not care about the nation and economy."[1]

Kim Jong Il first became involved with politics at 17 years old. To prove his loyalty to his father, the young Kim studied important political issues that were critical to the elder Kim. He advised and helped his father appoint and dismiss key party officials, and actively purged Kim Il Sung's personal enemies.

In 1973, Kim Jong Il successfully secured his position as a party organization secretary, a position initially meant for his uncle Kim Young Ju.

Ever since his rise to power, Kim has used propaganda to create amazing stories about himself. Construction engineers claim that the dear leader has taught them to decide where, when and how to build a dam. Fighter pilots improve their skills on takeoffs and landings from Kim Jong Il's instructions, which are posted in the control towers.[2]

While his people worship him as a god, others see a different side of the leader of North Korea. Kim Jong Il is an eccentric playboy who likes wine, women, and Hollywood movies. He often parties throughout the night, spending entire weekends in a suburb of Pyongyang with his favorite officials and a group of half-nude women known as "the Pleasure Squad." Kim also is crazy about European blonde babes. He loves their corn-colored hair, their deep-set eyes, and their large breasts. Under the name of social and cultural exchange, Kim has brought groups of German and Swedish prostitutes to Pyongyang.[3]

His bodyguard, Lee Yong Kuk, says he will never forget seeing Kim in a bathing cap splashing around his pool with a pretty nurse and a beautiful doctor at his seven-story pleasure palace in Pyongyang. The building contains a bar, theater, and karaoke machine. The two women swam around him, massaging his hands, legs, and back, and whispered into his ears.[4]

Kim Jong Il prefers foreign-made products. In his villas in China and Russia, all items must be imported from abroad, many from Japan. The staff in his office spends time on the road looking for exotic specialties to buy him. To hide his luxurious lifestyle from his people, who lack basic necessities such as food, Kim Jong Il makes public appearances during the early morning hours (usually between three and four). His tactics have obviously worked, as his people believe he is working diligently for them.

In South Hwanghae Province, Kim Jong Il has built a secret cattle farm. Many road checkpoints have been set up to prevent people from entering the farm, which is surrounded by mountains and a lake. People's Army veterans and their young wives and children live there to take care of Kim's cattle. They dwell in modest houses equipped with television sets and refrigerators. They cannot meet with their relatives and friends at home so they see them at the checkpoints while the guards watch them. Although they lead a solitary life, Kim Jong Il provides them with food, cooking oil, and sugar. They can also buy beef at low prices.

To ensure the finest-quality beef, Kim's cattle eat nutritious and natural feed mixed with medicinal herbs and live in a clean environment. Sick livestock are butchered and disposed of at once.[5]

Kim also enjoys baked donkey meat. And when Korean food becomes boring, he eats Western. In April 2001 Kim Jong Il imported two Italian chefs, paying them good salaries and allowing them to fly with their wives into Pyongyang. The two chefs prepared clandestine banquets of pizza for Kim Jong Il and his party of military elites. The cooks complained that the army generals confiscated their passports during their three-week stay in a barracks and monitored their every movement as they taught the Korean chefs the secret of rolling dough into thin crusts. When they bade farewell to their hosts, the Italians felt as if they had been liberated from a "golden prison."[6]

In September 2001 Kim Jong Il stunned the world with his lavish train trip to Moscow. He brought some 150 people with him, including doctors, cooks and top officials. Japan custom-made his armored train, which functions like a mobile five-star hotel equipped with the most updated facilities, such as satellite television. The train was powered by two locomotives; the first one served to eliminate mines and other obstacles. Of the 21 carriages, no one knew which car belonged to Kim Jong Il.[7] The train can run at 180 kilometers an hour, but for the purpose of safety, ran only between 30 and 40 kilometers per hour on the trip across Russia.

Throughout his journey of two weeks, Kim never saw the eager Russian journalists or the welcoming Russian people, not even Koreans living in Russia. At his request, the Russian government shut down the railroad stations along his route. One day, his express arrived at Novosibirsk. A woman in her eighties waited on the platform. She wore holiday attire and a pair of new shoes. Her hands held a picture of her husband, who had saved Kim Il Sung's life when he led a guerrilla force in the Far East during the Second World War. Everyone expected that Kim Jong Il would meet with the widow and renew the historic friendship. The train stopped for twenty minutes at the Novosibirsk station, but Kim Jong Il never appeared. Instead, a representative gave the anxious Russian lady a big suitcase full of gifts, including a picture album of scenic locations in Pyongyang and other places. Tears streamed down her heavily wrinkled face. No one knew if they were tears of gratitude or disappointment.[8]

Kim Jong Il turned sixty in 2002. Although he is healthy and highly energetic, he has long been planning for his eldest son, Kim Jong Nam, to succeed him as North Korea's future leader. The rumors of this had circulated as early as 1994, when Kim Jong Il became the country's top leader. Only thirty-one, Jong Nam now works in the public security department (police), the first step to becoming a national leader.[9] His mother is Chong Huei Lin, formerly an actress who moved with her parents from South Korea to Pyongyang in 1948. Her first husband was a physicist. They divorced after she and Kim met, and Kim married her in 1971. During the great famine of 1993, Chong, who is sixty this year, moved to Moscow and has settled there. Jong Nam, the couple's only son, followed his father's footsteps, studying in Russia and other European countries from the age of ten. One of his teachers said that he is clever and exceptionally good at philosophy. Few in the outside world, however, know who he is, for Jong Nam conceals his identity and tells people that he is the son of a North Korean ambassador. He enjoyed the easy life studying abroad, but in 1998 he returned at the request of his father. Jong Nam resembles his father in appearance. He has a round, soft body, a moon-like face, and a small mouth. Like his father, he also keeps a low profile in public. The young man spends money freely and loves women, often traveling abroad with female companions. Last May, Jong Nam, who wore a Rolex and carried Louis Vuitton bags, tried to enter Japan with a false Dominican passport, which he reportedly purchased for $2,500.

Kim Jong Il is very close to his little sister, Kim Jon Hui, the only sibling who has the same mother as he. Jong Hui now heads the light industry division of the Economic Audit Department. Kim Jong Il demands that the party and the country treat his little sister the same way they treat him. Her son Jong Hui and his little sister Jong Nam are the only two people Kim Jong Il will see at any time; only they can enter his villas freely.

Kim Jong Il always feels paranoid and needs heavy security. Indeed, there have been numerous assassination attempts, but he has somehow managed to thwart them all. Now, he has established a brigade of bodyguards to protect him, some 1,200 soldiers under the direct control of a lieutenant general of the People's Army.[10] Their duties are not only to protect the supreme leader, but also to crack down on any possible military coup.

Whenever Kim Jong Il appears in public, Office No. 6, the department in charge of Kim's security troops, deploys five circles of guards for his safety. Five or six guards form the first circle and escort him everywhere. These men must be full colonels with 25 to 30 years of service in the People's Army. Next, 200 to 300 guards form the second circle. The third circle watches the

Kim Jong Il with his son Kim Jong Nam and the family of his little sister, Kim Jong Hui (Xinhua News Agency).

area one kilometer in radius from the second circle. The fourth circle is responsible for an area of one-and-a-half to two kilometers beyond the third one. Finally, the fifth circle is composed of men from both the Events Sections of the National Security Agency and the Ministry of People's Security.

Kim's bodyguards live a life full of tension. They have to be ready for an emergency at very short notice, often being notified only two hours or even 45 minutes before hand of Kim's schedule.[11]

During their ten-year term of service, they cannot go out or take a vacation. Married officers can go home only once a week. But in return, these bodyguards enjoy treatment matched only by the party secretaries.

Inside Kim Jong Il's Friendship Hall, a hostess in a fresh orange gown stands in front of us, telling touching stories about the dear leader. But North Koreans, while shouting "Long Live Kim Jong Il" with passion, actually know very little about him.

Since the North Korean government does not want us to meet with ordinary citizens, we are sent to the Friendship Hall in the early morning, when both halls are almost empty. But upon our leaving the place in mid-morning, we pass lines of other organized groups of army soldiers, school children, and peasants from the collective communes. They remain quiet and express nothing.

Soldiers in the People's Army are only in their mid-teens. Their wide-rimmed army caps in their hands, the soldiers expose their crew-cut hair, looking even more haggard. They are poorly nourished, even though they receive larger rations than ordinary civilians. While the residents of

Pyongyang get only 200 grams of grain per person per day, and people in other cities and provinces none, the soldiers receive 800 grams of food every day. Even so, this is far from enough for these youngsters. They have to perform all kinds of military and civil assignments, such as harvesting crops, repairing dams, building roads, preventing disasters, patrolling in villages and arresting unruly citizens.[12]

When hungry peasants are too weak to plant crops, the army takes up the task. Soldiers cut trees in the mountains to build terraced fields, toil in mines and factories. The People's Army soldiers do not look healthy; obviously, they also suffer from malnutrition of various degrees. When the government was forced to reduce the soldiers' meager ration at the peak of the famine in 1997, many soldiers could hardly move or see as hunger weakened their eyesight.

Early next morning, Guide Kim knocks on our doors one by one to wake us up. Outside, the fresh air is filled with the smell of the pine trees, and the sound of the waterfalls in the valleys around our hotel. On the lawn, tiny beads of drew have formed on the grass. Several peasant women squat in the gardens, picking out weeds silently. In the parking lot, I am surprised to see quite a few Mercedes and BMWs.

I look further. On the stone benches by a fountain in the front garden, several older couples sit chatting. The men wear white sportswear and new sneakers. The ladies are dressed in tailored pants and flowery shirts. This is the first time I have seen ordinary North Korean women wearing such delicate, colorful clothes since entering the country. A young hotel assistant stands by, lighting cigarettes, offering a cup of tea, and giving a helping hand if needed.

A few more fashionably dressed couples file out of the hotel and join the group. Presently, these old men and women separate from each other and regroup themselves based on gender. They seem like healthy people, their faces glowing with natural redness. Unlike the gray-faced North Koreans around them, their bodies show no trace of starvation. In fact, some of the men's bellies protrude slightly. When they walk, their steps are casual and deliberately slow. Their postures are graceful as some of them climb into the luxury cars. BMWs and Mercedes Benz are symbols of their high-ranking status in the Korean Workers Party. Only political bureau members can qualify for a 328 model Mercedes; those of the central party committee only get a 280 model.[13] These cars are free, compliments of Kim Jong Il.

High-ranking officials live in comfortable living quarters composed of two spacious apartments. They frequent the few good restaurants and nightclubs in Pyongyang, which serve such delicacies as Argentine steak,

A Mercedes parked in front of a foreign exchange store in Pyongyang. Kim Jong Il awards each member of his political bureau of Korean Workers Party with a luxury car. Although allowing his subordinates to live lavishly, he never trusts them.

Italian Pizza, Starbucks coffee, and French red wine. They can go to foreign exchange stores and buy imported merchandise such as DVDs and VCRs, which ordinary North Koreans have never heard of.

Although he allows his subordinates to throw money around, Kim Jong Il does not trust them. He suspects that these people are the most likely to lead an uprising against him, so he monitors them closely, much more than he does ordinary citizens. He installs bugs in their homes and offices. These officials, living in constant fear, worry about how to survive each day. For them, "Serving the king is like sleeping with a tiger."

High-pitched songs resound in the early morning air: "Our blood is hot and boiling! We will always fight with you, our great General Kim Jong Il...."

Marching to the rhythm, three young woman soldiers walk shoulder-to-shoulder on the road leading to the mountain. Long guns on their backs, they carry ammunition and meals in their hands. Their hair is tucked inside their wide-rimmed army hats, and their serious-looking faces glow with youthful luster. The brown army uniform fits well on their petite bodies. My camcorder follows them. But the well-trained soldiers sense at once that they are being watched. They turn their heads back toward me, one after the other. During the decades of war preparation, many young North Korean women have abandoned their traditional roles as wives and mothers to join the Army.

The sun rises from behind the diamond-shaped hotel. A new day is unfolding. Once in a while, a bicyclist passes by, carrying cloth bags at the back of his bike. Leaning against the vehicle smoking, our driver has completed washing the bus. Guide Kim walks out of the hotel and gives us the order to get on board.

We head toward Pyongyang.

7. Pyongyang — Hell and Paradise

I choose a first-row seat in the bus to have a full view. After the sudden death of Kim Il Sung, Kim Jong Il ordered a four-lane highway to be built in 1996 to link Mt. Myohyang, the Kims' mountain resort, with the capital. Along the road, green mountains with brown patches of terraced fields mark the landscape. Clear water flows in the streams. The air smells new and the land is clean.

The Koreans' name for Korea is Choson, or "Land of the Morning Calm." It has also been traditionally called Koryo, "High mountains and beautiful rivers." White is the people's favorite color, signifying purity. For this reason, many wear white clothing. The Koreans are also good at singing and dancing. They love the seesaw and the swing. Men are well known for wrestling, and the women for their ability to carry heavy loads on their heads. Planted in the household yards, and growing wild in the mountains, the Rose of Sharon bush is everywhere. This national flower represents the people's indomitable spirit.

Huge political slogans attached to the mountainsides call upon the people to participate in the socialist construction. Red flags fly over the rice paddies. Organized groups of peasants labor with their bare hands. They have no spades, no hoes, only the most primitive of plows. They work slowly; starvation has weakened their resolve. In the collective communes, peasants earn the same work points and the same wages, regardless of how much effort each individual puts in. After the harvest, the state takes away the entire yield. Every year, North Korea needs eight million tons of grain. But the unmotivated peasants can produce only 2.5 million tons.[1]

Located in East Asia, North Korea is a small country, roughly equivalent in size to Mississippi. The land area of the entire Korean Peninsula is 1,500 square kilometers, containing a population of 70 million. The peninsula is hilly with many deep, narrow valleys. The rivers are often short but swift. Throughout Korea's history, natural disasters have been common. Severe flooding often follows late spring droughts.

The new highway is almost empty. Only once in a while, old military trucks pass us. These make up two-thirds of all the traffic. But the obsolete Soviet-made vehicles cannot run far. They often break down because of flat tires. The country has a serious shortage of rubber, which has to be imported, but the debt-ridden North Korean government is unable to afford it. Every few kilometers, at the roadside, military personnel surround their stricken truck, using rudimentary tools such as bicycle pumps to resuscitate their tires.

Ragged pedestrians walk in twos and threes, almost always with a soldier. People are not allowed to move freely from one place to another. If they have to make a trip, they must apply days ahead for a travel pass.

Groups of children picking weeds along the highway smile and wave at us. Children are educated to welcome Chinese travelers, but to show contempt to people from other countries, especially those from the West.

Our bus driver honks at the poor pedestrians. Some of them watch us with envy. Others, hopeless about the long trip ahead, wave to hitch a ride. In their eyes, the bus driver is the most powerful man on earth. If he would only be kind enough to stop, he could save them days of walking. Even though our bus is only half-full, it continues to bypass people signaling for help.

"We cannot allow people to be on the bus with foreigners. This is our national policy. Violators, including the hitchhikers, the driver, and even myself in this case would all be severely punished," Guide Kim explains.

While the most beautiful young women work as showy police officers in Pyongyang, wearing miniskirts and directing traffic that does not exist, the less comely ones serve as hostesses in the International Friendship Halls and five-star hotels. The middle-aged and elderly peasant women crouch along the roadsides, picking weeds and collecting trash. In the collectively owned fields, women carry babies on their backs, separating seedlings and digging for wild grasses to mix with wheat and corn powder for food. Older children play at their mothers' feet, dirt covering their twig-like limbs.

North Korea has always been short of men to farm the fields. Today's ratio is two men for every three women.[2] Kim Jong Il made the situation worse by turning North Korea into a military kingdom, with an army of

Kim Jong Il reviewing his one-million-strong army (Xinhua News Agency).

over one million. Wherever we go, I see soldiers, in the village entrances, on the highways, in the mountain valleys and fields. If a high school graduate cannot get into a university, then the army will be his life. This leaves the North Korean women to do all the farming. Lack of manpower, pesticides, and fertilizers, plus the lasting natural disasters, all contribute to the starvation.

The North Korean government forces women to raise as many children as possible and bans abortion. Once war starts, the country will need men to fight. But few women want to give birth to more than two children. Life is already harsh enough since mothers have to worry every day about feeding their children. Many infants are born underweight. Eating grass soup with a few grains, babies cannot survive. Their painful cries cut their mothers' hearts. It is not uncommon for a woman to first drown her small children and then kill herself to escape hunger.

In general, North Korean women are treated as second-class citizens, born to serve men.

"I don't do anything at home," Guide Kim says, "I have four daughters, and my wife raises them alone." When asked what would happen if his wife failed to please him, he replies that he simply does not go home and spends the night in his office until she repents and asks him for forgiveness.

It is almost noon. The sun moves atop the steep mountains. Soldiers carry picks and spades, dragging their legs, trying to walk in formation. Their uniforms are stained with mud. Young mothers hold the hands of their children and hurry forward, hoping to reach their destination before night falls. A policeman in white coat and blue pants stands on guard every few kilometers, checking the passersby.

Presently, Pyongyang appears above the horizon. Its name meaning "a piece of flat land" in Korean, the capital was constructed under Kim Il Sung as a paradise on earth. When he was alive, he ordered trees to be planted everywhere so Pyongyang would look like a big park. The city now has only two factories, and even they are near closure.

The streets are cracked and seriously deteriorated. People crowd at each bus stop, waiting patiently for the limited trolley, old East German trains decorated with their unique graffiti. The rattling trolleys are the only means of transportation in the city for civilians. The advantage of these vehicles, Guide Kim says, is that they do not use tires, thus saving these precious resources for military vehicles.

As if by decree, every person keeps to the sidewalk; no one crosses the streets. That seems very unusual for a capital city with over two million people.

"If you see someone crossing the streets, he must be a People's Army soldier. Only he can do it because a soldier often has an emergency and is allowed to do so. No one else can," Guide Kim explains.

Richard Lister, a BBC reporter who came to Pyongyang to cover U.S. Secretary of State Albright's visit in 2000, heard a siren that sounded dawn, noon and midnight to signal work, eat, and sleep. At 8:15 every morning, he saw an all-girl marching band in blue uniform playing loud patriotic music on Pyongyang streets to cheer people up as they started a new day. However, Pyongyang citizens "seem ground down by the sterility of the place. They walk in silence, unsmiling.... Pyongyang feels like a slightly shabby communist theme park—a sort of Leninland, but Leninland at closing time with only a few people drifting the streets and the lights going out."

On the streets, only men ride bicycles. Women are forbidden to do so because the government orders them to wear long skirts, and exposing their legs in public is not graceful and hurts the country's socialist image. The building of the capital has long stopped. Not one new structure is under construction, and not a single truck transporting goods or merchandise can be seen. In the distance loom two tall chimneys, which belong to the only power plant providing Pyongyang's electricity. In recent years, production has dropped sharply, and power outages are a daily occurrence.

Pyongyang.

In 1986, U.S. satellite pictures taken at night showed Pyongyang radiating with lights. But today, when I look at the city from my hotel room on the 14th floor, it is enveloped in pitch darkness. No lights on the main streets. No lights from the rows of residential buildings. The only thing shining is the red torch burning on the Juche Tower, standing across from our hotel and representing the ideology of national isolation and self-reliance.

People in other provinces have already lived a life without electricity at all for many years.

On the bus, Guide Kim's voice rings again through the microphone in his hand: "This is a hospital...." He points to a dreary-looking building of concrete blocks. The gate is closed. Pyongyang's hospitals, and hospitals everywhere in North Korea, are horrible. Telephones there do not work, so asking for help in an emergency is difficult. All of them lack medicine, even basic supplies, and suffer from frequent power outages.[3] They do not serve regular meals. Mothers refuse to send their sick children to the hospitals because the tender ones can contract pneumonia in the heatless rooms during the freezing winter and malaria during the summer, when mosquitoes and other pests infest the wards.

The factories no longer produce medicines. And the government,

Opposite: The tower of Juche, symbol of self-reliance. At night, only the torch still shines in the lightless city of Pyongyang.

already heavily in debt, cannot purchase foreign drugs. In the hospitals, nurses and doctors often steal even the small amounts of medicine available, to sell for food in the black market. Only those who have money can afford pills. Most people have to go search for herbs in mountains.

German Doctor Norbert Vollertsen, a member of Doctors without Borders, entered Pyongyang in July 1999. While treating a workman who had been badly burned by molten iron, he cut skin from his own thigh to be grafted into the patient. For this, the media hailed him as a hero and awarded him the Friendship Medal. He was allowed to travel to many areas inaccessible even to many North Koreans.

In a children's hospital, he saw "crude rubber drips hooked to patients from old beer bottles. There were no bandages, scalpels, antibiotics or operation facilities, only broken beds on which the little ones lay waiting to die." The children were too small physically for their age. Their eyes were sunken and their skin tight across their faces. Their blue-and-white striped pajamas reminded the doctor of children in Hitler's Auschwitz concentration camp. They were so weak and malnourished that he was afraid that flu could kill them easily.

In 1998, UNICEF and other UN agencies estimated that about 800,000, or 38 percent of North Korean children under five suffered from malnutrition, especially those who lost or had been separated from their parents.[4] These vulnerable children are chronically malnourished, suffering from stunted grown both mentally and physically. It is a ruined generation.

A North Korean man tells of his sad experience in a Pyongyang hospital. "The hospital has no medicine. It is a hospital in name only. It is no more than an inn for people to stay there just temporarily. When I was sent in, I looked like a beggar and the doctors didn't even look at me. I could not eat or drink. Everyone said that I would die within two or three days. Doctors were unwilling to give me even an injection of dextrose.

"I soon remembered nothing. Then one night in the darkness I heard water dripping. The clear sound knocked on my ears and brought me back into the world. I asked in a weak voice, 'Water please! Water please!'

"I was very thirsty and my throat was smoking. Getting no answer, I crawled with all my strength toward the water sound. But I was stopped by something. I opened my eyes. I saw a corpse wearing nothing at all. Lying side by side were all corpses...."[5]

However, in Pyongyang there does exist another type of hospital, equipped with the latest medical apparatus, such as magnetic resonance imaging, ultrasound, electrocardiograms and X-ray machines—as German doctor Vollersten discovered when he got inside one of them.

Elite college students carrying Soviet-style school bags near the country's most prominent Kim Il Sung University in downtown Pyongyang.

Indeed, two worlds exist in the capital city: a paradise for the senior military and party elite and a living hell for the rest.

While most of Pyongyang looks like a big slum with obsolete buildings and rundown sheds, the central government buildings and surroundings look quite orderly. The structures are magnificent, with gigantic statues and revolutionary monuments around them and political billboards on top of their roofs. Not far away are An Sang Taek and Munsu Streets, where some of the top government officials dwell. Sons and daughters of the privileged wear Western suits and Nike canvas shoes; they smoke American cigarettes like Marlboro and Mild Seven. (A pack costs 100 won [$50], almost an entire monthly wage for workers.) They frequent bars and restaurants where only foreign currencies are accepted, spending hundreds of dollars on food, Starbucks coffee, and soft drinks. Jealous children of other high-ranking officials living on Changgwang Street show off by cruising the Pyongyang streets in their fathers' Mercedes sedans. They use U.S. dollars to buy luxury goods in Pyongyang's diplomatic stores. The elite no longer sing North Korean revolutionary songs, which they say are out-of-date. Instead, they listen to classical music and South Korean pop.

There are other signs of affluence and indulgence in Pyongyang. Officials own flat-screen televisions shipped from Beijing and spend vacations in Thailand and Australia while millions of their countrymen lack food, clean water, electricity and all other daily necessities.[6]

In Pyongyang's biggest department store, only pencils, exercise books with coarse, darkish, repeatedly recycled paper, plastic Korean shoes in the shape of small boats, a few China-made bicycles, and sewing machines are on display. No one knows whether they are just for show or are really for sale.

8. *In the Shadow of Juche*

Our bus stops in front of the Friendship Tower, a monument erected in the heart of Pyongyang after the Korean War to commemorate the Chinese Volunteer Army soldiers. Neither Americans nor Chinese can forget this cruel carnage, which lasted from 1950 to 1953. One-third of the U.S. army, one-fifth of its air force, and half of the Marine Corps fought in the Korean War. The Chinese fielded more than one million soldiers. It was one of the bloodiest wars in modern history.

In front of the Korean Revolutionary Museum stands a colossal figure of Kim Il Sung at 23 meters tall. The statue was originally painted gold, but the color was removed after visiting Chinese leader Deng Xiaoping severely criticized this excessive act of personal worship. Tremendous slabs of concrete decorated with gigantic statues idealizing the Juche doctrine flank Kim's statue. One can find such massive monuments everywhere in Pyongyang.

The North Korean government protects its pride carefully, sometimes even at the cost of money and lives. In Pyongyang, there are many things that are "number one in the world." The Juche Ideology Tower is one meter higher than the Washington Monument in the U.S. capital. The Arch of Triumph in downtown is twenty meters higher than the one in Paris, upon which it is based. Pyongyang's gymnasium can hold 200,000 people, although it has been used but seldom. Pyongyang also owns the world's tallest hotel, at 102 stories high. Built with picks and shovels, the high-rise has already slanted and is sinking.

During his visit to Pyongyang, British journalist Jasper Becker was shown a hospital full of unused new equipment produced by Siemens. In

This gigantic statue of Kim Il Sung, once painted gold, stands downtown in Pyongyang.

The North Korean version of the Arch of Triumph, which is twenty meters higher than the one in Paris. Although the capital of a poor country, Pyongyang boasts many of the world's "number one."

The Pyongyang Hotel, in the shape of a pyramid, is the world's tallest hotel at 102 stories. Built with picks and shovels, the high-rise is already slanted and sinking.

fact, even the plugs still had plastic wrapping on them. As gifts from the Great Leader, they cannot be used. In the deserted shops that lined the streets, modern Japanese cash dispensers and plastic vegetables were stacked to the ceiling.

A local female guide, dressed in a hanbok, greets foreign visitors in front of the Arch of Triumph. She smiles and poses for our pictures. Without my knowing it, road blockades have been set up around the monument to prevent the local people from getting close to us. Policewomen stand at the intersections. These women in their early twenties wear Soviet-style broad-brimmed hats, white shirts, and light-blue miniskirts. They have very smooth complexions, big black eyes, long eyelashes, and full lips. Trained not to show their feminine charms, the girls look straight ahead, their bodies as stiff as a rod, their facial expressions serious. Waving the traffic stick in their hands, they turn in different directions every now and then although the streets are empty, with almost no vehicles and very few pedestrians.

Not far away, in the heart of the city, is Kim Il Sung Square. A line of schoolgirls in straw hats and white shirts are practicing group aerobics for the 50th anniversary of the country's founding, which is to take place on September 9th, 2001. Despite the ongoing famine, the government spends a lot on the celebrations. National Day, Anniversary of the Workers Party, Birthday of the Great Leader, and Birthday of the Dear Leader include

A North Korean woman in colorful national dress decorates the city of Pyongyang like a flower.

hours of carefully choreographed demonstrations of mass adulation. In October 1997, the entire population of Pyongyang was mobilized to celebrate the half-century anniversary of the Workers Party. On February 17, 2002, the government ordered everyone in Pyongyang, North Korean and foreigner alike, to participate in at least one activity such as a concert, rally, or parade to commemorate Kim Jong Il's sixtieth birthday. Those who refused suffered punishment as criminals. At least 100,000 youth danced to the marching music, performing mass aerobics shows. At night, parades of one million people blocked the Pyongyang streets. Asked how they could keep their positions in total darkness, they replied firmly, "Our dear leader has prepared everything for us. He is the lighthouse in the darkness. All we need to do is to follow his instructions and the road always lies ahead of us."[1]

On the face of Mount Kumgang is a message, "General Kim Jong Il, you are our illustrious commander!" Each word is 34 meters tall and 2 meters deep, visible for miles. The North Koreans use a calendar system based on the Juche year. The first Juche year starts with the birth of Kim Il Sung.

Manyongdae is the suburb of Pyongyang where Kim Il Sung was born. Lavish trees and trimmed lawns surround these well-kept farmhouses with golden thatched roofs. Rice bowls, chopsticks, pens, books, clothes, and farm tools that Kim and his parents and grandparents used are on display.

North Korean travel guides setting up a road blockade in front of the Arch of Triumph in Pyongyang to separate us from the ordinary North Korean people.

According to government propaganda, Kim Il Sung came from a dirt-poor family, but he was not overcome by poverty. When still young, he went to study in China's Jilin Province, where he learned to speak fluent Chinese and joined the Chinese Communist Party. He led a group of guerrillas to fight against the Japanese in the Changbai Mountains (Mt. Paektu), therefore being recognized as the friend of the Chinese people. During the years of war, he established the Democratic Republic of Korea, and his guerrillas have grown into today's one million–strong Peoples Army.

Not far away is a well that Kim's family once used. Colorful plastic cups sit on a nearby rack. Visitors taste the well water and remember the kindness of Kim Il Sung.

Ironically, some of the many trees around this area, in somewhat less conspicuous locations, have been stripped of their bark. Suyi says Pyongyang people boil the strips of bark and drink the soup or grind them into powder to be mixed with other synthetic "food."

Under Kim Il Sung's Juche guidance, "everyone is systematically starving together." Tony Hall, an American congressman from Ohio, sees evidence of slow starvation on a massive scale: "Families eating grass, weeds

Downtown Pyongyang is almost empty. Movement, including crossing the streets, is strictly controlled.

and bark; orphans whose growth has been stunted by hunger and diarrhea; people going bald for lack of nutrients; and hospitals running short of medicine and fuel.... Even the military is suffering. The soldiers' uniforms hung off their bodies."

Still, Manyongdae, to the North Koreans, is a sacred pilgrimage site. Every day, school children and other citizens come to worship Kim Il Sung and pledge loyalty to him. In North Korea, Juche is the country's sole religion. The government severely restricts other religious beliefs, saying that "no one can use religion as a means to bring in foreign powers, or to disrupt the social order."

According to North Korean government, there are several Buddhist temples and churches— two Protestant and one Catholic — in Pyongyang. However, church activities are for show and Christians who attend services without approval from the government land in solitary confinement. Terry Madison, an American religious leader, says that about 50,000 Christians nevertheless live in North Korea. They meet in secret house churches. Kim Jong Il's army conducts house-to-house searches for them. "Whoever has a bible in hand is accused of being a spy — anything connected with the outside world means arrest and death."

North Korean secret agents have even extended their searches to China's border. In April 1999, a 58-year-old North Korean Christian man

Primary school students taking a break on Kim Il Sung Square during their mass gymnastics practice for the coming celebration of the Dear Leader's sixtieth birthday.

living in Yanji, China, disappeared. A month earlier, two South Korean missionaries had been murdered in their home, together with four North Korean Christians.[2] The U.S. State Department estimates that the North Korean government executed about 400 Christians in that year.

Most of the visitors to Manyongdae are young Koreans. They look serious and prayerful. Separated from the rest of the world, the eight million young people, one-third of the entire population, have their own way of entertainment. Like youngsters elsewhere in the world, they love singing and dancing to "capitalist cultural trash": karaoke, rock-and-roll, and techno; but the government bans these. Instead the government sees to it that songs like "The March of General Kim Jong Il," "The Thunder at the Summit of Jung-i," and "Our Youthful Blood is Boiling, and Our Heart is Burning like Fire" are played. Officials also permit some light-hearted old folk songs such as "City Girl Get Married," and "A-ri-lang" (handsome young man).[3]

Kim Jung-soo, Lee Fen-jee, and Lee Jin-soo are some of the famous female celebrities that sing praises to the leaders:

> Rose of Sharon
> Is blooming only under the golden sunshine.
> I, like a Rose of Sharon,
> Can grow
> Only under the sunlight of the glorious Workers Party.

A massive celebration in Pyongyang for the 55-year anniversary of the Korean Workers Party (Xinhua News Agency).

> The Party is like my great mother,
> Nurturing me with her great Juche.
> Oh, Juche is a shining beacon in the darkness,
> The warm sun in a cold winter.
> Follow the Party, we will march to victory.
> Follow Juche, we will have a tomorrow of prosperity.

North Korean youth also like fashion. In Pyongyang, young men wear sunglasses and western suits. Women perm their hair, apply makeup, and wear high-heeled shoes. But jeans and shorts are prohibited. Skirts must be below the knee. Chinese fashion still heavily influences North Korean youth, who grew up watching Chinese movies, listening to Chinese revolutionary songs, and using goods imported from China. Similar to the situation in China's Cultural Revolution, hairdressers and beauty salons

Manyongdae, the birthplace of Kim Il Sung on the outskirts of Pyongyang; a must-go place for the North Koreans, especially the young people, to worship.

in Pyongyang can only provide basic services such as cutting, trimming, and shaving. Anything more is still banned as capitalist rotten lifestyle.

The park by the Daedong River is a great dating place. There, young men and women snuggle together under the trees. Young North Korean women love dating People's Army soldiers, many of whom are children of peasants. The military not only provides these poor boys with a bigger ration of food and clothes for all seasons, but also gives them favored treatment in transportation, lodging, employment, and medicines.

It is almost noon, and my stomach is grumbling. I could not eat the pickles we had for breakfast, so I left the dining room hungry. I am excited to hear that we will have mudfish soup, a local specialty, for lunch. The restaurant is located on the ground floor of a downtown hotel. The interior decoration is impressive. Passing the glass dividers, I feel I am entering an art museum. Engraved patterns of various shapes and traditional Korean paintings of mountains and rivers decorate the walls. Soft lights shimmer in every corner. White cloth covers the tables and the backs of the chairs are carved with dragons and flowers.

We are invited into the kitchen to see how the mudfish soup is cooked. The kitchen is very clean; the tall windows are bright and counters free from grease. The chef performs dramatically. He kills the mudfish, cleans it, and cuts off its head. Then he cuts the fish in two and puts the chunks into hot-water jars. When the water begins boiling, he skims the foam, adding garlic, salt, pepper sauce, and green onions. He lets the soup boil until it becomes creamy. A dozen stone cookers send out white steam along with the fragrance of the mudfish in them. Then, the charming waitresses place on the table a jar of soup, a bowl of rice and a plate of kimchee. The soup looks purple in color, with red pepper floating on the top. Sitting against green onions and white Tofu, it looks just like a piece of art.

There is a story behind the mudfish. The North Koreans have never liked the fish before. Why has it become so popular now? The chef tells us that the Dear Leader Kim Jong Il knew that Pyongyang residents would love to have fish instead of other alternative food all year long. So, in 1996 he started a campaign to raise mudfish nationwide because, like potatoes, the fish survives easily since it eats only mud. It grows fast and will produce food cheaply. In years of famine, people cannot afford to be picky and would eat anything. The chefs are also creative. They have invented many ways to cook the mudfish. In this restaurant alone, there are 35 methods: the fish can be boiled, fried, baked, sauced, salted, preserved, or steamed....

9. *Pyongyang's Everyday Life*

Downtown Pyongyang lacks commerce of any sort: few department stores and shopping centers, no neon signs, posters, or commercial billboards. The only airport in Pyongyang is as big as a mall's parking lot. American tourist Simon Bone described it this way as his plane landed in the country: "We caught our first glimpse of the North Koreans as the plane was landing. It looked like they had temporarily ceased wandering across the runway, as if stopped at a pedestrian crossing for aircraft. The landing strip lay in the middle of a much-used dirt road."[1] Every week, only ten passenger airplanes take off and land in Pyongyang airport.

Buildings in Pyongyang, blackened by the weather, have not received any maintenance for many years and seriously need repairing. Other than Kim Il Sung University, Party Headquarters, and some luxury apartments nearby on Changgwang Street, most places look drab and rundown. The capital seems as if it has been devastated by war, and only the Kims' portraits, revolutionary posters, and red banners hanging from the structures color the overwhelming grayness.

"President Kim Il Sung is the never-setting sun!"

"Long Live Juche."

"Long Live the Great Korean Workers Party!"

Pointing to a square-shaped, ten-story building on Kwang Fu road, Guide Kim says proudly that his home is on the seventh floor. He emphasizes again that all Pyongyang residents enjoy free housing and he pays nothing for the 120-square-meter apartment.

In a typical Pyongyang living complex, I see housewives gathering at the security office. Guide Kim says that these women like gossiping: which

People's Conference Hall in downtown Pyongyang.

girl has a male visitor today; who buys a fish this morning; a boy in Room 403 has been mischievous at school and received a warning. Crowded living conditions permit no privacy so quarrels are common. But neighbors do help each other. Only a handful of dwellers own refrigerators, but they are willing to share them. People help watch each other's sick children and old parents.

In these apartment buildings, elevators and other household appliances oftentimes do not function because of power shortages. The water supply is disrupted all the time. Washing clothes and cleaning the toilets have become problems. Instead, residents use portable water, which is available for only one or two hours a day. So, in the complex courtyard, people form long lines to get water from the public faucets. Some have to carry buckets of water up many flights of stairs to their rooms, which can be as high as the tenth floor. Those living on Munsu Street even fetch water from the Daedong River.

Residents also have to carry bicycles, the sole means of transportation for common people in the city, all the way up the stairs where elevators do not exist or have broken down.

Without heating, Pyongyang's apartments resemble "prison cells" during the severe winter. The rooms are cold because many windows have no glass or any covers. Families wrap up in quilts, trying to keep warm in subzero temperatures. Looking from outside, these apartment buildings appear empty and lifeless. Only those on Changgwang Street for the ranking party officials show signs of life: at least their windows are covered with plastic paper.

On New Year's Day and February 16, Kim Jong Il's birthday, the government provides "Benevolent Heating." But many Pyongyang residents cannot even enjoy this benefit, because obsolete gas pipes, unused for a long time, are blocked, cracked, and very unsafe.[2]

City residents raise chickens, rabbits and pigs on the balconies. While staying in Pyongyang, I am awakened in the morning by the crowing of roosters at an apartment building near our hotel.

The residents who live in Pyongyang's deteriorating apartment buildings must be politically reliable. Those who have foreign liaisons, including Chinese relatives, can only live outside the city. The government strictly controls who can and who cannot live in the capital, since food, housing, health, and general living conditions there are superior to those in the rest of the country. Under the guise of population control and war preparation, the government periodically drives "politically impure elements" or "unruly people" out of the city.[3]

Pyongyang Subway lies one hundred and forty meters underground. It is the biggest and most splendid in the world. The interior is dazzling, with built-in lights on the walls and a great mural of Kim Il Sung beckoning and smiling aloft at his people with workers and peasants in the background. The lavishly-built subway is not practical, since even the roads above are almost empty. It is constructed solely to boost the ego of the national leaders. Even during the rush hour, not many people use the subway. With one guide leading the way and the other tailing the group, we step onto the long escalator. I do not know whether plain-clothes policemen are watching, but people seem to understand that they are being monitored. None of them look at us. As everywhere we go in North Korea, silence prevails. People do not talk to each other. Even babies keep their mouths shut. Once we step off the escalator, I look around to make sure no one is watching me. I take out my camera. But before I lift it to my eyes, a hand coming out of nowhere pats me on the shoulder. "Please put away your camera. You cannot photograph people."

It is the pleasant-looking cameraman, who seems to be smiling all the time.

We sit in an empty carriage between two cars that serve local passengers. Through the windows, the North Koreans steal glances at us.

In the late afternoon, we stop at the Pyongyang City Theater to watch an acrobatic performance. In front of the building, elementary schoolboys,

Built for show, the gorgeous Pyongyang subway is almost empty year-round.

dressed in white shirts and black slacks, are participating in a drill. Each boy holds a long club, practicing one-to-one combat. When they tire, they sit or squat on the concrete near the bushes. Everyone must stay together. No one is allowed to wander away from the group or walk about freely. Every week, the North Korean children must do several hours of mandatory war-preparation training.

Outside the impressive theater, organized groups begin gathering. The North Korean citizens can watch the performance for free, but the activity must be monitored. There is no freedom of movement. Our group, along with the haggard soldiers of the People's Army, takes precedence over anyone else. A few people from the other groups follow us, but the ushers guarding the gates scold them and shove them aside. It is hard to watch these pleasant-looking women in traditional colorful gowns acting so ferociously toward their own countrypeople.

In the theater the first center rows are reserved for the soldiers. This

Pyongyang citizens in the world's largest subway system.

is one of the privileges that the military enjoy. Watching acrobatics with foreigners is another political task for the armed men, who have been relieved of other duties for the day. The soldiers all sit straight in their seats, projecting a good image of the People's Army to the foreign visitors.

The enormous theater fills quickly to capacity. Stirring music resounds in the air. An image of a huge Rose of Sharon is projected on the screen. Brilliant lights radiating from the flower symbolize the glorious warmth and great kindness of the dear leader. The scene shows the world that life is normal in Pyongyang, that people in all walks of life are happy and love the socialist North Korea. Amid the high-pitched, thrilling music, performers in bold silky costumes holding high the flags of the Korean Workers Party and the Democratic People's Republic of Korea march onto the stage, waving enthusiastically to the audience. The Koreans are renowned for their acrobatics, which are supposedly the best in the world. But today the performers' ability seems to fall short of their expectations. They fumble constantly, dropping this and missing that. A big and tall man who is supposed to let others climb onto his shoulders to form a human ladder cannot stand back up under the weight. He tries several times, his face sweaty, his legs shaking, but still fails. He is weak. His job requires a large quantity of good food. Apparently he does not get enough.

Several Korean mountain bears also give a performance. They are so

A gigantic mural of Kim Il Sung surrounded by workers forms the background of the Pyongyang Subway.

slim and small that their size approaches that of an average dog in the United States. To conserve their energy, trainers have the bears do small tricks such as throwing balloons, turning somersaults, and kowtowing to the audience. They do not jump ropes or push carts around the stage, their traditional performances.

The last act is the flying trapeze, which marks the climax of the show. Ladders, long thick ropes, and other equipment hang from the vaulted ceiling. Then the performers stretch out a sturdy net one meter above the stage. Music starts playing, and the performers call out Kim Jong Il's name. The audience holds its breath as the acrobats fly back and forth in midair from one side of the stage to another. A rainbow of lights sweeps the theater from the performers to the audience. A girl stands at the edge of the ladder, her body moving to the rhythm of the song. A young man behind her holds one of her arms. She is ready to fly. Suddenly, all lights go out, and the theater turns dim. Another power outage.

The power plant in Pyongyang has fallen short in its production of electricity; the blackout has certainly interfered with all daily activities, including the surgery rooms of hospitals. Only underground military facilities and the light of the Juche tower operate as usual. The government guarantees the military emergency supplies of electricity, water, and gas.[4]

Outside Pyongyang City Theater, young students receive combat training while waiting to watch an acrobatic show. No one is allowed to stray from the group.

The performers remain calm, kicking their legs, and moving their arms as if still performing. Their spirits are dampened however, and the disappointed audience sits quietly. But, no one jeers or shows any dissatisfaction.

After fifteen minutes, the electricity still does not come back. The performers begin jumping one after another from the ceiling ten meters high onto the big net below. Accustomed to the frequent power outages, they have already prepared for their exit. Now I understand the special use of the huge net. At the moment, it is a life-saver.

Even during this emergency, the performers still try to maneuver their bodies gracefully, pretending this is just a part of the acrobatics.

The People's Army soldiers and our group are the first to leave, followed by the rest of the crowd. Outside, it is pouring. Black Mercedes limousines pick up several senior men and speed away. The obsolete army trucks with full loads of "baby soldiers" roar as their ancient engines start. After they leave, we return to our comfortable, Japanese-made buses.

The North Korean audience, children included, stand in their respective groups, waiting for the storm to stop. Repressive quietness prevails except for the sound of the rushing rain, which quickly accumulates into huge puddles on the deeply cracked pavement.

"The uncanny muted atmosphere of Pyongyang and its citizens" has bothered many international visitors, who call the unusual hush "unnerving."

10. Underground Casino

Our hotel in the capital city of Pyongyang is one of the few open only to foreigners. Nevertheless, it has no foreign news satellites or other Western amenities. In the lobby, Kim Il Sung and Kim Jong Il stare down at us from a huge mural. It shows Pyongyang in the background, with the two leaders walking over a bridge. The father is giving lessons while the son listens and takes notes. As we check in, a handful of foreign visitors from India, the Middle East, and Europe roam the lobby, surrounded by plain-clothes men.

After dinner, I realize that I have to charge my camcorder in preparation for our next day's trip to the DMZ at Panmunjom. But all the sockets in my room are British-style. The clerk at the front desk tells me to go to the basement, "Usually, you need approval to go down there. But since you are our Chinese friend, and you have an emergency, please feel free."

The elevator takes me deep into the basement. When the doors open I feel as if I am in a different world. Neon lights flash, elaborate light fixtures glow, and large chandlers dangle. The rooms are decorated with redwood furnishings. Modern pop music fills the air. A young girl in a red silk gown, embroidered with dragons and flowers, greets me. Tall, handsome security guards patrol the halls. Foreign diplomats float in and out.

A middle-aged woman in a black suit embraces me. Holding my hand tightly, she introduces herself as the manager. She says that she and her employees have come from the border city of Dandong in China. Meanwhile, the curious eyes of the courtesy girl and the security guards never leave me. Their desperate hunger for human contact and friendship is overwhelming.

81

"What is this place?" I ask.

"This is a casino owned by a man from Macau. Businesses of this nature can only operate in the basements of large-scale hotels. They are meant for foreigners, not North Koreans," the manager explains. Then she and the others start eagerly to ask me questions:

"We are so glad to see you. Which places have you been to?"

"Did you come alone?"

"Are you used to Korean food?"

"How do you like the people, the country?"

Bombarded with questions, I feel confused.

"We are like prisoners down here," the manager finally confesses.

"Why?" I am shocked.

"For two years, we have been stuck down here. We are not allowed to go upstairs. And people upstairs are seldom allowed to come down except for these diplomats, who come here to gamble. The North Korean government regards this as a dirty place that poisons the pure minds of its citizens. It thinks all foreigners are just capitalist trash, craving nothing but money, sex, and drugs."

Entertainment, gambling, dancing, and singing Karaoke take place only in the basement. The manager and her employees can neither leave the hotel without permission nor reveal their identities. They sleep here, eat here, live here and work here. Once a month they can go out as a group to sightsee. But Korean interpreters always accompany them, keeping track of how many people go out and return.

As the manager explains this to me, the employees nod in agreement. The lady continues: "They open and read our letters. We can take almost nothing out of the country when we visit Dandong, not even a newspaper. They search us all the time. But we have a way. We hide stuff in pillowcases and underwear."

She looks at me and asks, "Why did they allow you to come down here?"

Before I can reply she says that hotel guests are frequently locked in their rooms and go nowhere without official company. The government does not want foreigners to get to know the common North Koreans. It does not allow its own people to talk to each other, either. No one can move around without a travel pass. Everyone is watched.

"Don't you see the soldiers patrolling on the streets? There are many more in plain clothes. We are discriminated against here simply because we are foreigners, 'ideologically poisoned and morally rotten.' The North Korean government does not care about us. What it cares about is whether or not we are approaching their citizens and telling them about what is happening outside North Korea. The situation is still not good. Food rations are tight and people are dying at this very moment."

It is hard to believe that a massive famine is actually taking place in North Korea. Ever since I entered the country, I have never seen "hordes of refugees," or "corpses by the roadside." Other visitors say the same thing: the disaster in this country does not resemble any other famine.

Why?

North Korea's Public Security Agency and the National Security Bureau (secret police) strictly control the people's movements. On September 27, 1997, after Kim Jong Il's party secretary, Hwang Jang-yop, defected, Kim ordered all of the 210 counties to set up the "927 camps" to detain those who stray outside their villages or cities without proper documentation.[1] The Stalinist-style permit system keeps people in their home villages most of their lives and effectively limits their movement. Furthermore, people cannot receive their food rations unless they remain at home. Since September 1998, the government has prohibited citizens without both travel permits and train tickets from getting on trains.

In Pyongyang, designed as a showcase city, controls are even stricter. One can not speak loud, laugh, sing, dance, party in public, or loiter, spit, even cross the streets at will. No children are playing. People in Pyongyang wear dull colors and drab clothing. The Party's ideological control over everyday lives is total. Public self-criticism is held if a worker returns one minute late after lunch. Speaking to foreigners is absolutely forbidden. A woman who flirted with one was put to death on City Square.

"The official xenophobia was such that a Korean girl who tried to marry a Syrian and leave the country was executed in a public stadium," British journalist Jasper Becker wrote after his visit to North Korea.[2]

Ordinary people have no idea about the outside world. To ensure that the people can hear no second voice, radios and television sets in North Korea are built only to receive domestic programming; foreign-made shortwave radios must be altered. Listening to foreign broadcasts is a crime that results in death. Private telephones cannot make or receive international calls. Mail is censored.[3] Although Kim Jong Il loves the Internet, it is not available to ordinary citizens.[4] Only the government agencies and certain party officials can access it. The North Korean media paint a horrible picture of the rest of world, while depicting their own country as an oasis of prosperity and happiness.

Generations of children have been taught that the words and deeds of the Kims are the absolute truth. North Koreans say that they will serve as bullets and bombs in defense of Juche. They shout "Hail to Kim Jong Il," believing that communism will surely be realized on their soil under the leadership of their dear leader. Even college students, although opposed to isolationism and preferring reform, have never openly criticized Kim Jong Il and his policies.

To protect the honor of socialism, many people would rather die at home than on the roads. Besides, the government would not let anyone die by the roadside. That is why this famine looks different than any other.

Holding hands, the lady manager and I talk for two hours. Before I say goodbye to her, the manager gives me a few telephone numbers and asks me to call their homes when I return to China. Their eyes linger as the elevator doors closes behind me.

Back in my room, I turn on the TV. Only one channel is available, although Guide Kim has said that there are two, one needing "special skill" to locate. On the screen, workers appear in dust-covered clothes using electric drills. The camera lingers on the drills from all angles. Women work with sewing machines in crowded workshops. Plates holding dark-colored steamed bread and cakes stored in a glass food case keep flashing on the screen to assure people that food is available. Pointing to the plates, an official is talking to a reporter, constantly praising Kim Jong Il whenever he mentions them.

Following the long interview, the news switches to a classroom. Standing in front of a portrait of Kim Il Sung, a primary school teacher delivers an emotional speech to wide-eyed children. She instructs the children to love the great leader even more than they love their parents, for no one can live a happy life without him.

North Korea provides compulsory education for all children until the age of 15. Worshipping the two Kims is the major function of all schools, which use Kim Il Sung's 27 volumes of Juche ideology as the core curriculum. Ideological dogma even fills the mathematics textbooks: "A worker could make only 10 spades in the past. But after he listens to our dear leader Kim Jong Il's speech on National Day, his productivity has increased dramatically. Now he can make 15 spades in a month. How many more spades has the worker made now than before?"

In teaching revolutionary history, literature, and geography, the teacher writes the answers on the blackboard to avoid making serious political mistakes. The students must remember the year and other details of Kim's history. To please the government, the teachers show discrimination in grading tests and papers, giving extra points to those students who choose military service and taking off points for those who want to enter colleges.[5]

Kim Jung Il likes only healthy and beautiful children, whom he, like his father, holds up for photographers. The leaders deny children with disabilities or from politically problematic families health, education, and social services and do not allow them to live in the cities. Every two or three years, the leaders drive these unlucky children out of Pyongyang and send them to the remote mountains where camps have been set up to prevent them from "multiplying," as Kim Il Sung once said.[6]

At 11:00 p.m., the TV station signs off. It is totally dark outside. Buildings, streets, and rivers all look murky. A curfew goes into effect after dusk, allowing no outside activities. There are no signs of commerce, no voices, not even the honking of car horns one would expect in a capital city of over two million people. Pyongyang looks like a desolate graveyard of concrete. I check my door. It is locked from the outside. I lie in bed hoping that the night will pass quickly.

The next morning Guide Kim pounds at our doors to wake us up. After breakfast I remember that I have left the charger to my camcorder in the basement, so I once again take the elevator. I do not call for permission this time, since I already know the way. As I step out of the elevator I am alarmed to find myself in complete darkness. I turn back at once, trying to get back on the elevator, but the door has already shut. I am very nervous. It is deadly quiet here. Where are the beautiful girls and the handsome men? The woman manager? What has happened to the neon lights and the lively music? She has told me that they all live down here. But now, the huge gambling place looks like a deep cave. I begin shouting, but no one answers me. Filled with fear, I pound the elevator door, and repeatedly press the button.

"I will be trapped down here. The guide has no way of knowing where I am. And today, they will leave for Panmunjom. And I will be stuck here…."

As my eyes adjust to the darkness, I see a thread of light coming from the end of a tunnel. I fumble toward it. Suddenly a groan, coming from a dark corner, startles me. I stop and look. Slowly, a man rises from behind a sofa.

"I am looking for the charger to my camcorder, which I left here last night," I say in Chinese.

The man turns on the table lamp by the sofa. In the dim light, I see his drawn face, messy hair and wrinkled shirt. The man stands up and walks toward the socket where the charger is still plugged in. He unplugs it and gives it to me. Sitting on a chair nearby, he stares at me humbly. Looking at his protruding cheekbones, I take out two hard boiled eggs left from the last meal and hand them to him. He shakes his head and looks away. I offer again.

"No, not eggs. Do you have…" he puts two fingers in front of his mouth and puffs.

"Cigarettes?" I ask.

"Oh, yes," he replies shyly.

"I don't smoke," I feel sorry that I do not have cigarettes to offer him. China's Yunnan-brand cigarettes are sold at a steep price in the black markets and are indispensable in North Korean society. Giving a pack to the train conductor or bus driver, one can earn a free ride from one city to another. Giving a pack to a patrolling border guard, one can cross over the river into China. At a critical moment, a pack of cigarettes can mean life or death to an ordinary Korean.

The young man looks very disappointed. But he takes the eggs I have offered him and puts them into his pocket. To save electricity, he turns off the table lamp, and the basement becomes dark again. Silently, he accompanies me to the stairs before disappearing into the deep cave again.

When I emerge from the basement into broad daylight, everybody on Bus Number 2 is waiting anxiously for me. Guide Kim has looked for me everywhere.

Looking at the blue sky that stretches as far as the eyes can see, I am happy to have gotten out of the "gorgeous prison" where my new friends have been locked up for almost two years for no reason at all.

11. The DMZ

Panmunjom is a small border village divided by the Demilitarized Zone (DMZ) between North and South Korea. It is our last destination before we leave North Korea. After this visit we will head back to Mt. Myohyang for the night before taking the train to Ji'an in China the next morning.

From Pyongyang to the southern border, the land is flat, planted with neat rows of crops. On the horizon tall mountains rise, dotted by clusters of whitewashed villages. Korean farmers never use flat lands for their homes. They build their houses right at the foot of the mountains or on their slopes, yielding every inch of flat land for farming. Food is always their first priority.

After traveling for two hours on the almost empty highway, our bus enters North Korea's second largest city, Kaesong, 35 kilometers from Seoul. The zone between Kaesong and Pyongyang is the country's most highly developed industrial area; Kaesong is nevertheless a bleak sight. Only one tall smokeless chimney rises from the city. The roads are in terrible shape. The unpainted, neglected buildings along the streets are poorly maintained. Most of the windows have no glass. The sky, the pavements, the summer willow trees, even the propaganda banners all merge into one gray color. Flocks of crows wheel in the air. Some try to fly into the open windows.

Pedestrians in thin white clothes walk silently in the fine rain without umbrellas or raincoats, their eyes fixed on the flooded ground. Skinny children with red scarves around their necks and Soviet-styled school bags in their hands hurry along in small groups. Even in the city center, streets

are deserted, with almost no automobiles in sight. Only a few male bicy-
clists in round-rimmed straw hats glide along the slippery roads.

Other than the humming of its engine, our bus is deadly quiet. We
are awed by the poverty of the country's second largest city.

Guide Kim's voice rings out, "Kaesong is a very sensitive place. International espionage agencies like to sneak into the city to collect information. Please do not take pictures. Anyone who violates this rule will be
detained."

The short man's usual soft smile has disappeared. His eyes sweep
sternly across the seats while delivering his message.

The man sitting behind me reacts, "I am sure you have a lot of spies,
especially those from South Korea."

He touches on a sensitive topic that others try to avoid. "I am an obedient man, never taking pictures when you ask us not to," he starts praising himself. "But not every one behaves as well as I do. Some people still
take pictures secretly and are interested only in recording poor places,
hungry people, and the dark side of society," he adds.

My spine freezes. The man sitting behind me is a member of the Chinese secret police from Jilin Province. Once, when I accidentally men-
tioned his identity, he appeared startled and hushed me with his finger to
his lips, "The North Koreans don't want to hear this."

Now, feeling threatened by Guide Kim, he has tried to divert attention from himself.

I am now very afraid. Guide Kim turns his head towards me, the only
one in the travel group who carries both a camcorder and camera. His
small eyes carry a light of suspicion.

"May I ask what you are doing in China?"

My heart jumps fast.

"I teach at a college," Blood surges into my head.

"Which college?" He quickly follows up.

"Xuzhou Railway University," I make up the name.

"I have never heard of it."

"It's near Nanjing, a big city by the Yangtze River," I try to reply in
a calm voice.

"Why do you come to our country?" He narrows his eyes and looks
at me closely.

I feel a lump forming in my throat. Why did I carry a camcorder into
this country? Am I not asking for trouble? In Ji'an and other cities along
the Chinese border, those carrying a camcorder are usually travelers from
South Korea. Even there, I am taken as a South Korean tourist, and the
locals often speak Korean to me.

Today, from the moment we boarded the bus, Guide Kim has sounded threatening. He even tells us that although people like him are just travel guides, their suggestions, and the information they gather from their work, can reach the top in a minute, leading to swift reaction. The travel guides are core members of the Workers Party, the eyes and ears of Kim Jong Il's regime. Brainwashed for years, yet receiving the best of everything, they are ready to sacrifice their lives to protect the Party.

I am having to justify myself to him. "I am a teacher on an assignment. I came here to learn what a genuine socialist country is like because China is no longer a real one. I will tell my students what I see here when I come back."

"So, what is your impression of our country?"

"It is much better than I first imagined. For example, it is very clean here. And your cities have a lot of trees and people work hard...."

I speak the Shanghai dialect, the same dialect as he. His Chinese language teacher is a volunteer soldier from Southern China. He has often complained, "Like teacher, like student — that is why I can't speak the Beijing Mandarin like those young guides."

With my reply, Guide Kim's face relaxes into a subtle smile.

"No matter what happens to us, we will stick to the socialist road to the end and will not take any other way. This is our strong belief and no one can break it even if the world alienates us. We have been isolated long enough already."

As our bus passes through the streets of downtown Kaesong, the driver becomes impatient, honking the horn to disperse the sparse pedestrians, who run to the sides to yield the road. Guide Kim finally turns his head away from me and begins talking to the driver in Korean. I must be very cautious for the rest of the trip. What if they find out that I am from the United States? If Guide Kim becomes suspicious of me, it could be dangerous. I force myself to remember that tomorrow will be our last day. The dangerous trip will soon end.

I will never come back, I tell myself. Searches, interrogations, threats, and the wax-like boiled cabbage and endless pickles are too much for me. I have never felt so confined physically. And my fellow tourists agree with me. "Why are they so afraid?" We ask each other.

It is about 10 o'clock in the morning when we arrive at a compound close to the Demilitarized Zone south of Kaesong. Facing the gate is an imposing propaganda poster with two schoolgirls holding doves. A North Korean girl wearing a green dress with a red scarf smiles innocently. Another girl, beaming in pink, represents South Korea. The poster is a call for unification, the lifelong wish of Kim Il Sung, who wanted to be the president of a united Korea. Like his father, Kim Jong Il believes that he can conquer the South someday by means of force.

Although he clearly understands the economic disparities between the two Koreas, Kim Jong Il feels confident about his huge army. He once told party secretary Hwang Jang-yop that in case of war, he would use artillery bombardment to destroy Seoul in five or six minutes. Then his armored troops would launch a general offensive throughout the South. They would occupy Pusan and seal off the entire peninsula before the Pacific forces of the United States had time to intervene. Kim Jong Il trusts that missile attacks on several Japanese cities, including Tokyo, will stall any U.S. support to South Korea.[1]

Kim Jong Il regards his People's Army as the "vanguard of unification and the only hope for the state," and asks that "everyone support the military to the utmost."

Kim Jong Il worships Adolf Hitler, who died rather than surrender. Kim once declared, "The world does not deserve to exist without the Democratic People's Republic of Korea, and should the nation implode, we will take the rest of the world with us."[2]

Most North Koreans believe him. They call the South Korean army "scarecrows" and "pushovers." They say that death through battle is more glorious than death through starvation.

The compound where we are waiting is four kilometers from the DMZ. It consists of only one major building and a few low sheds at the sides. Cement, gravel, sand, and other construction materials litter the ground. It is surrounded by a no-man's-land of brown earth and hard rocks. Soldiers of both sides can carry only pistols. They are allowed no heavy weapons. To get to the border, we will take a ten-minute bus ride and pass through numerous military checkpoints.

Seven or eight bare-chested soldiers are repairing the roof of the major building. A couple of them are taking a break, their legs dangling from the eaves while measuring us silently from the top. Several military jeeps are parked at the back of the complex. I stroll over. Looking inside one of the jeeps makes me shudder and jump back: two soldiers sit motionlessly with machine guns in hand, their eyes looking ahead, never blinking, at the people in the compound. Their stiff posture shows that they are ready to act at any moment. As if nailed to the ground, I feel difficulty in moving.

I am stunned: the compound is not as casual as it appears. I forgot that this is only minutes away from the world's most hostile border, and the no-man's-land that encircles us is laden with mines. No one dares to enter the zone without a military guide.

For decades war preparation has been the North Korean government's

板门店

The DMZ — the world's most heavily armed border. Picture tken from the North Korean side. The building is occupied by American soldiers.

top priority. After he became Supreme Commander of the Korean People's Army in December 1991, Kim Jong Il supervised the construction of military facilities and participated in every area of military planning. Under him, North Korea makes all its munitions, helicopters, ships, missiles, and rocket launchers. Pyongyang, the headquarters of the Fifth Corps, has underground fortresses with living quarters for all the soldiers. It has state-of-the-art lighting, water, and ventilation systems. Electricity is always available there, compounding the power shortage that Pyongyang people face every day.[3]

Since even the elite Korean People's Army suffers from starvation, the Party forces ordinary people to give their rationed food to the military and records their donations as a measure of personal loyalty. Thus, donations among people, especially junior officials, are ferociously competitive.

Although the starving army cannot exercise often and its weapons are obsolete, it still poses a threat simply because of its size. Consisting of over one million men, it is growing "closer and deadlier." It is reported that the People's Army continues to deploy some 4,000 tanks, 2,000 armored personnel carriers, 13,000 artillery pieces, and 160,000 troops at the border with South Korea, which has only half as many soldiers and weapons, backed up by 37,000 American troops.

CIA deputy director John McLaughlin warns, "North Korea's artillery could rain havoc down on Seoul. It has the biggest pool of special forces in the world, not the best, but with enough punch to sow panic and destruction.... For the United States, North Korea is—first and foremost— a challenge."[4]

In the parking lot, two German tourists guarded by two "interpreters" look at my camcorder as if wondering how I am allowed to bring it into the country. But we can only look at each other briefly. A free conversation is impossible. We know that numerous eyes are watching us from every hidden corner. Any movement without permission is illegal here.

There are many Germans in the country. Germany formally established diplomatic relations with North Korea in March 2001, the eleventh member of the European Union to do so. Historically East Germany, as a member of the Soviet bloc, provided North Korea with weapons and technology. It trained North Korean students and engineers and sent in its experts in electronics, textiles, railroads, and other scientific fields. Since German unification, however, North Korea has cut many ties with its former ally, although it still allows limited numbers of students to study in German universities.

An hour has passed and we are still waiting for an officer who will "escort" us into the DMZ.

"Please be patient," Guide Kim says. "Since we have so many visitors today, the officers are in high demand." But I have not seen many tourists. Ordinary North Koreans cannot travel here, much less escape across the southern border. No one can easily pass through the countless military checkpoints, set up on the roads along the highway from Pyongyang to Kaesong, from Kaesong to the DMZ, and from the DMZ to the South Korean border. All vehicles, including ours, must stop frequently to undergo questioning and searching. Pedestrians will be stopped even before they leave Kaesong.

Soon a special bus enters the parking lot. A North Korean officer comes out of the building at once to meet it. The gate leading to the DMZ opens to let it pass. This bus belongs to the Chinese Friendship Delegation, consisting of high-level government officials, who have been sent to North Korea for field study.

Another half an hour passes before an officer finally shows up and summons us to get on the buses. Only with him on board can the soldiers along the six checkpoints in no-man's-land allow us to pass.

On the border, neatly trimmed lawns and artistically shaped bushes and trees, blooming with huge purple and pink flowers, surround several

The negotiation table in the house at the DMZ.

well-kept one-storied houses. Inside the first building, I see a long table covered with green cloth. This is the room where the ceasefire negotiations took place during the Korean War. History comes alive here. In June 1950, North Korea invaded the South, which had only 98,000 troops equipped with small guns. The North Koreans fought with 135,000 Soviet-trained troops and one tank brigade. Just a few days later, Seoul fell.

A United Nations force, led by the United States, intervened. After the Inchon landing of October, which caught the North Koreans completely off guard, U.S. troops drove the People's Army out of South Korea and penetrated deep into the North, capturing Pyongyang. When Stalin declined to join the war, Kim Il Sung, who had been a veteran Chinese Communist Party member and a soldier in China's war against Japan, wrote to Chairman Mao Zedong, begging for help. At the Korean War museum in China's border city of Dandong, Kim Il Sung's hand-written letter to Mao is displayed.

"We have to ask you for a special assistance as the enemies are approaching our territory north of the 38th Parallel. We urge you to send the Chinese People's Liberation Army to fight shoulder to shoulder with the People's Army. We are looking forward to your advice and instructions."

China, barely recovered from the wounds of its own decade-long warfare with Japan and the Nationalist Chinese, was still eager for another confrontation. There was strong disagreement from many top military leaders, including Marshal Lin Biao. Lin did not think that the Chinese Army could beat the Americans, who were equipped with modern technology and powerful weapons. However, Mao, inflated by his overwhelming victory in China's civil war, promised Kim that although China was experiencing its own economic difficulties, he was determined to fight the American imperialists. He would send out troops to stop the Americans before they took Pyongyang. He believed that a war now was better than a war later and appointed Marshal Peng Dehuai as the general commander of the 1.2-million Chinese Volunteer Army that came to North Korea. Mao entertained Marshal Peng at a family dinner and told the general that his newlywed son, Mao Anying, would also want to go to North Korea. Marshal Peng was hesitant. He knew what it meant for a young man to fight in this dangerous war. Anying begged and Mao supported him. Before Mao saw Marshal Peng off, he raised the wine cup and toasted,

"I wish you two success in North Korea."

Marshal Peng understood that he could only win.[5] What unfolded was one of the bloodiest wars in modern history. By December 1950, the Chinese army had pushed the international troops into the South, re-taking Seoul before they were driven back to the 38th parallel. With the participation of the Chinese army in the war, about four million people on both sides lost their lives. Altogether about 360,000 Chinese soldiers died or were injured.[6] Among those dead was Mao Anying, the eldest son and designated successor to Chairman Mao Zedong. The young soldier was eating lunch when a bomb exploded outside his shelter. Anying was buried in a village, where his body remains to this day.

The United States spent about $830 billion on the war. At the end, the American casualties numbered 50,000.[7] My nextdoor neighbor, Jay, was a disabled Korean War Veteran. His infantry participated in several famous battles. In his words, "The most horrible thing was that when the fearless Chinese soldiers were charging, they just rushed to us wave upon wave like an ocean. They were endless. You even had no time to refill the ammunition."

Another red-brick house sits on the border between the two Koreas. In fact, the border cuts right through it. This was where the two sides signed an armistice agreement almost fifty years ago. The microphone on the negotiation table separates the two Koreas. This is the only room where one can be in North and South Korea at the same time. Tourists from South Korea can also visit. However, the dates on which visitors from each side are allowed alternate. On this day, the door leading to South Korea is shut.

During the Korean War, Kim Il Sung (right) met Marshal Peng Dehuai, the commanding general of the Chinese Volunteer Army. (Xinhua News Agency)

Placing himself at the front of the room, the army officer with hollow cheeks starts speaking in a high-pitched voice. He talks so fast that Guide Kim can hardly follow along, and no one can understand the translations. From the soldier's tone I guess that he is condemning the enemy while singing high praises to Kim Il Sung.

Behind the windows of the signing room are tidy barracks in light gray and sky blue. The North Korean soldiers stand still at their respective positions. These men, strictly selected, are of the same height and same weight. Their frozen faces resemble statues carved from rocks.

Although the North Korean government keeps its soldiers ignorant of the truth about South Korea and the outside world, the men stationed at the border do have an opportunity to look at the South. During the day, they see streams of cars moving back and forth. At night, an ocean of lights brightening the dark sky astonishes them. None of their southern counterparts look hungry. They appear strong, healthy and well trained. The North Korean soldiers know at the very bottom of their hearts that South Korea is richer than the North. After dusk falls, when they look behind them, they see the lifeless darkness where their families live.

However, with endless brainwashing and no access to information, the soldiers believe they must "safeguard the socialist country with the last drop of blood." They support Kim's unification policy and believe that

The house in the DMZ where the cease-fire negotiations took place in 1953.

they must achieve it by any means necessary. The American troops must pull out of the South. Otherwise, war is inevitable. The People's Army, the most alienated group of all the population, eagerly seeks war. They are confident that socialism is superior to capitalism. They remember the words of their general commander, "We possess nuclear and chemical weapons. With them alone, we will surely win."[8]

However, secretly cherished in every soldier's heart is the delusion that once the two countries are unified, "we can eat the fine rice produced in South Korea's Cholla Province and its delicious meat soup."

South Korean National Defense Minister Kim Dong-shin has stated that North Korea now owns 5,000 tons of chemical and biochemical weapons, including anthrax and smallpox and one or two nuclear bombs.[9] It is also working on new models of ballistic missiles. Defense Secretary Donald Rumsfeld warns that these missiles, known as Taepo Dong, are capable of striking California: "Weapons of mass destruction pose risks to not thousands of lives but hundreds of thousands of lives, when one thinks of the power and lethality of those weapons."[10]

After the September 11 attacks on New York City, the North Korean media publicly stated that the incident was tragic and that innocent civilians should not have been killed. The government announced that it would cooperate with the international community in the fight against terrorism, but condemned the United States for "unilaterally resorting to a violent retaliatory war" in Afghanistan.

彭德怀在朝鲜战场

Chinese Marshal Peng Dehuai during the Korean War (Xinhua News Agency).

In private, however, the North Koreans have expressed admiration for the September 11 attack. The government has ordered its military personnel to emulate the Middle East terrorists by engaging in new terrorist operations cheaply.[11]

The house where the cease-fire agreement between China/North Korea and the United States/UN was signed in 1953. A subsequent peace treaty has never been signed, however. Officially, the two sides are still at war.

In the DMZ, ten meters away on the other side of the barracks, American soldiers stand side-by-side with their backs facing the North Koreans. At 12 o'clock sharp, both sides begin changing guards. The Americans retreat into a grand building meters from the barracks to take a nap. The South Korean soldiers, dressed in light gray uniforms, come over to take their place. A new group of People's Army soldiers goose-step in line with raised chests, swinging their arms vigorously in midair.

As every country must have its right to wage a civil war, the true tragedy of the Korean War is "not the war itself, for a civil conflict purely among Koreans might have resolved the extraordinary tensions generated by colonialism and national division. The tragedy was that the war changed nothing: only the situation prior to the war was restored. The tensions and the problems remain unsolved."[12]

Officially the Korean War has not ended, since a peace treaty has never been signed. Today the confrontation between the two sides continues. About two million heavily armed soldiers from both Koreas, plus U.S. troops, still face each other every day. War can be triggered at any time.

For example, in November 2001, North Korean troops fired three machine-gun rounds across the border, breaking the window of a South Korean guard post. South Korean soldiers fired back. The incident

Gigantic revolutionary monument commemorating the Korean War in downtown Pyongyang.

occurred just hours after President George W. Bush criticized North Korea's weapons program. This was the second border incident in two months. In September 2001, North Korean soldiers had crossed the border, and the South Koreans fired warning shots at them.[12]

I can feel the highly intense atmosphere here. President Clinton, alarmed by North Korea's nuclear program, came to inspect the heavily militarized border. He called the DMZ "the scariest place on earth."

I want to take pictures, but our North Korean guides pressure us to leave. For some reason, they do not want us staying here long. They seem to have an unspeakable fear that we may see and learn too much. Our daily schedule has been kept secret. No one knows where we will really go until the bus starts running.

Returning through the no-man's-land, our bus stops at a row of barracks for lunch. Guide Kim insists that since the People's Army soldiers have prepared the food, we should taste it. In accordance with Kim Il Sung's Juche spirit of self-reliance, the troops not only guard the border, but also grow their own crops. The dining room is spacious and bright. The tables and chairs are clean. But the meal is boiled cabbage with noodles made from potato powder, lots of kimchee, and a few chunks of fatty pork. One glance at the food is enough to ruin my appetite. We have not had a "real" meal since coming to North Korea, and the travelers' faces look as haggard as those of the soldiers who provide the service.

After lunch the sky turns dark. It is going to rain. On our way back to Pyongyang, a long line of tractors is driving on the highway. Red flags surround the vehicles, and military trucks trail behind. The peasants are transporting potatoes the size of eggs from other parts of the country to the capital city. Rain pours down. The farmers escorting the tractors huddle under the plastic cover meant for the potatoes.

Near Pyongyang, organized crowds line the highway, with a policeman on guard every few meters. Huge loudspeakers placed on top of small cars shout out the good news: "Thank our peasant comrades for sending potatoes to us!" Braving the rain, people of all ranks in Pyongyang gather to welcome the potatoes. The wait for the potato tractors must have been long, for the fatigued children spiritlessly squat by the roadside, their wet clothes clinging to their small bodies.

In recent years, the government has become unable to guarantee the rice ration. Since 1998, the Korean Workers Party has called upon the peasants to grow potatoes because of the crops' ability to better endure natural disasters and for their relatively shorter growing cycle and higher yield. Kim Jong Il himself coined the phrase "potato is the same as rice" and inspected a model commune known as Big Red County many times. The *Worker's Daily* claims that Kim Jong Il "has lit the torch of a potato revolution" and predicts that the potato production for 2001 will be four million tons.[13] About one-sixth of the country's arable land will be used to grow potatoes.

In the official market potatoes cost less than 10 chun ($0.05) per kilogram, but they are strictly rationed. In the black market, the price can be as high as 30 to 40 won ($15.00) per kilogram. At foreign exchange stores, it is $1.00 per kilogram. Only those foreigners who work and live in Pyongyang can afford to buy these potatoes. For ordinary Koreans, one kilogram of potatoes in the black market would cost one third of their salary of 130 won ($60.00).[14]

In 1999, Kim Jong Il also initiated the "Exchanging Grass for Meat" campaign, announcing, "The Swiss use no grain but grass to raise cows and sheep. These animals eat only grass, but produce milk, meat, butter, and cheese, which will help alleviate our food shortages."[15]

In response farmers cut down trees and built fences on the mountain slopes. They built large goat farms across the country. In May 1999, Kim Jong Il inspected the Youth Goat Farm in South Hamgyong Province, where the famine had hit the hardest. Following his visit, the Agriculture Ministry organized children to collect weed seeds to feed the goats.

After Kim's inspection, the *Worker's Daily* trumpeted, "Once the development has been completed, we will have tens and thousands of tons of goat milk, butter, and cheese, not to mention the meat."

But goats do not thrive in winter. When the grass withers the animals turn to grains, competing with humans. With both animals and humans starving to death, the "Exchanging Grass for Meat" campaign has ended in failure.

In downtown Pyongyang, we stop to bow again in front of the massive statue of Kim Il Sung standing across from the government buildings. Then our bus heads back towards Mt. Myohyang. The silence is contaminating. In North Korea, I have learned not to talk, and now my lips seem to glue together. Some passengers close their eyes and others look out the windows. Gigantic political slogans carved in the mountains and erected in the summer fields jump into the eyes, loudly proclaiming the great victory of Juche. The farm hands, mostly women, cultivate collectively. Once in a while, boys soaking in the swift current running below the highway bridge wave at us.

Inside the bus, the thin but harsh voice of Guide Kim echoes, "If the United States were not against us, and if the Japanese repented of its historical crimes, we would have concentrated on our socialist development. We firmly believe that under the correct leadership of our dear leader Kim Jong Il, the day will surely come when everyone achieves communism, with abundant rice and meat to eat at every meal."

12. Out of the Prison Country

It is already late afternoon when we return to the diamond-shaped hotel nestled in the valley of Mt. Myohyang. I can still smell the trees and hear the creeks murmuring around me. The pointed glass roof turns pink and purple, reflecting the colorful sun setting behind the mountains.

In the revolving dining room, Guide Kim declares unexpectedly that after dinner we can enjoy karaoke on the second floor, gambling in the basement, and spa and massage services on the third floor — all at extra expense.

The insurance lady, who shares the hotel room with me, changes into a black dress dotted with small red roses and puts on a pearl necklace. She will dance with the two Chinese secret policemen tonight.

With no companion, I decide to stay in the room. I turn on TV, but again it is a blank screen.

We are scheduled to leave at seven the next morning, but the train arrives late again. We wait for two hours before we board our "special express."

The tedious journey begins—15 kilometers an hour. Still it is connecting and disconnecting with cargo trains loaded with timber and scrap metals to trade for Chinese corn. But these resources have nearly been exhausted. Since 1999, the import of corn has gradually declined, causing the price in the black markets to soar. Many cannot afford the food, and new deaths have occurred in the mountainous regions.

Inside the train, the same crew welcomes us again. I take my old seat opposite the young male attendant and put the camcorder on the small train table. The man seems shocked to see the equipment that every North

Korean links with espionage. He throws me a look to the side, then carefully picks up the camcorder, and turns it over to examine its every detail. In between, he raises his head and looks at me from time to time with questioning eyes.

The train rolls past broken bridges, houses without tiles, and dusty country roads. Hollow-eyed children in patched clothes stand at the village entrances and stare at us with numbed expressions. Little Wang, our Chinese guide, appears under the colorful portraits of the Kims, reiterating that taking photos along the way is strictly prohibited.

Suyi, the plump Korean-Chinese woman, stops by, and the North Koreans invite her to sit down. Without language barriers, they laugh and talk just like family members. The difference between the Korean spoken in China's Yanbian Korean Autonomous Prefecture and that in the North or even the South is as slight as American and British English.

Feeling neglected, I ask Suyi, "What are you talking about? Did you tell them that you went to South Korea and made a lot of money there?"

"Am I tired of living? Of course not!" She whispers back in Chinese. "These are no ordinary train attendants. They are all retired army officers with outstanding discharge. Every one of them, including the young girl, is good at using weapons and can fight well. Behind their laughter lie hearts of steel. Don't forget that one of their major duties here is to watch us. I can't wait to go back home. I don't want to stay here for one more day."

Our train passes a mountain slope marked by countless small patches of privately cultivated terraced land.

Suyi moves to sit next to me, saying, "The more we move towards the China border, the more small patches we will see. Rations have stopped long ago for people living in the northern regions. The government figured that people here can help themselves: find stuff to eat in the mountains, reach a deal with the food dealers roaming all over the border area or ask for grain from their relatives in China. In this mining district, big mines can still get food, but it lasts the miners for only 10 days a month."

But where does the international aid food go?

Before the severe flooding of 1995, Kim Jong Il had declined international assistance. He said that if the anti-Japanese guerrillas could fight by living on grass roots, then the North Korean civilians should be able to live on tree bark.[1] To Kim, national pride comes before lives. But, the increasingly acute starvation finally forced him to ask for aid in 1995.

However, with the coming of generous international food assistance, the ordinary North Koreans are still starving. Soldiers have posed as civilians, unloading ships carrying aid right under the nose of the inspectors from the United Nations. A North Korean woman living in a concealed apartment on the Sino-Korean border says, "My children couldn't go to school because rations had stopped completely. So, they went to the mountains to collect firewood, which they sold in the black market in exchange for food there. We have never received any foreign food, but I know it goes to the military first, then the hospitals."

American President George W. Bush confirmed the woman's accusation. He said in April 2002, "This kind and great nation [the United States] provides 300,000 tons of food a year to the starving North Korean citizens. Yet, the North Korean citizen has no idea that we provided the food. And we don't even know whether or not the food has gotten to the starving North Korean people."[2]

David Morton, the head of the World Food Program in Pyongyang, knows where the food aid goes: "At harvest time, the cooperative retains a year's supply of food, then the top groups including the army take a full year's supply. The remainder of the harvest is then distributed to the people through the public distribution system. So people have to make up the balance by all possible means, borrowing from relatives in the countryside, finding wild food on the mountainside or chopping wood and selling it."

Suyi now almost pastes her face on the window, obviously absorbed by the small patches of land. "I have been in and out of the country many times to see my uncle's family. No matter how bad the famine is, Pyongyang residents and the party organizations have always had their rations. And the police and the military always get the best. Ordinary people here are still miserable now but few have been starved to death as they had before."

She continues in a calm voice as if telling just a normal story, "Today, you don't see many kotchebi [fluttering sparrows, as orphans are called] begging and living on the streets. Why? Because people in this poor region must learn how to survive without the government, which has abandoned them long time ago. Look at these fire fields. Even adults who are not farmers have learned how to 'patch farm.' They no longer work wholeheartedly at work for the socialist construction but risk their lives to rush to their secret patches near their homes or in the mountains whenever they can to cultivate private crops. No one can stop them, not even the party secretaries. First and foremost, people must have food to eat. They must survive. Communist ideology does not work as well as before."

Although these people devote all their energy and "spare" time to taking care of the plants, the crops still look poor because of the lack of fertilizer.

"People suffer most in the first half of the year when food storage is almost exhausted and the new seedlings have just sprouted," Suyi adds.

"During this period of time, many will have nothing to eat although in the marketplace there is almost everything. I went there one time. The markets are as rich as the ones in our Yanbian. They have everything, you name it — fur coats, rice, dried pork strips, soy beans, sweet potatoes, salted fish and duck eggs, cans of all kinds. Most are from Jilin Province. The cans are American food. But most people couldn't afford the goods. The price is way too high."

"Hi, Mr. Handsome," the male attendant sitting opposite me greets a tall passenger who passes our seats. He is the general manager of a big company in Tianjin, China's third biggest city.

"Please interpret for me," the attendant turns to Suyi for help.

The Tianjin man, flattered by his praise "Mr. Handsome," smiles and humbly declines the praise. From his pocket, he takes out a box of expensive Yunnan cigarettes and throws it to the North Korean man.

"Thank you! Thank you!" The attendant deftly catches the flying pack.

"Do you get a lot of compliments from others?" the attendant continues to praise "Mr. Handsome."

"No, only from my wife."

I find the female attendant staring at my bracelet, which is made from fragrant wood and carved with images of Buddha. It is a good-luck charm. Although I feel a little reluctant, her desiring eyes melt my heart. I take it off and offer it to her.

"No! No! I can't take this. I'm just curious," she shakes her head. She is sincere. I put the bracelet on her smooth wrist.

"Would you give me your address so that I can send you the pictures we took together?" I hand her my scribble pad. The girl hesitates, then says, "Just send them to your guide Little Wang at Ji'an International Travel Service. He will relay them to me on his next trip."

Her cautiousness reminds me that a North Korean citizen cannot have personal relationships with any foreigners. If I contact her at her home, or send her things by mail, the young girl will lose her current job and be punished severely for violating the strict rules on foreigners.

Our train stops suddenly at a rural station. Huge portraits of Kim Il Sung and Kim Jong Il are the only decorations in the rudimentary setting. Several men in faded uniforms squat in front of the small waiting room, basking in the sun. They look at me, but their bony and bronze-colored faces show none of their inner feelings. The attendants are busy talking to Suyi, the plump woman, so I open the window. The men, panicked at sight of the camcorder, are briefly at loss for what to do. Covering their faces in shyness, they stand up abruptly, quickly entering the small station. They stare at me covertly from behind the windows.

A crowd is waiting anxiously but quietly for the tardy train. Many men and women carry on their backs luggage so heavy that the ropes penetrate deep into their muscles. Several armed security guards stand at the back, watching the crowds. Soon a broken-down train arrives, an old Chinese model. People in rags cover every inch of the train, even on its top, making the train almost invisible. Everyone carefully guards his own place and no one moves even if the safety officers dutifully order the crowd to come down from the train top. Watching them, I imagine their thoughts:

"We would rather give our lives than come down. We have neither an ID card nor a travel certificate. To obtain both the travel certificate and the train ticket, we will have to pay one month's salary. Standing at the threshold of death, who can afford to pay so much for a trip? We get on top of the train because we cannot get in through the windows. Just inches over our heads is the high-voltage cable that goes along the railway. If we touch it by accident, electricity will send us into the sky. The train top is not an ideal place to sit. But since the train has no schedule, we cannot wait at a station for two or three days. And no one knows how long it will take for us to go from one place to another...."[3]

After eight hours, our train moves into Manpo Station, where we are to change trains to China's Ji'an. "Mr. Handsome" and his colleagues pick up their belongings and go to the door. The long trip has saddened and exhausted everyone. At about the same time, the door is pushed open and a soldier jumps on board and blocks it with his arms. "Go back to your seats!" he yells at them.

"What are they going to do?" I hear Mr. Handsome and his group asking each other.

"Search! Did you forget?"

"This regime is weak," "Mr. Handsome" whispers, "I have been to so many countries around the world. Never seen anything like this. This is a very strange country, even stranger than ours during the crazy Cultural Revolution. It is so mean and so evil...."

I begin worrying about my camcorder tapes, films, and notes. All of them contain information that the North Korean government does not want the outside world to see or know. I remember the warning issued by the U.S. State Department before I left America:

> The Democratic People's Republic of Korea authorities may seize documents, literature, audio and video tapes, compact discs, and letters that they deem to be pornographic, political, or intended for religious proselytizing....
>
> The activities and conversations of foreigners in North Korea are closely monitored by government security personnel.... Pho-

tographing roads, bridges, airports, rail stations ... can be perceived as espionage and may result in confiscation of cameras and film or even detention. Foreign visitors to North Korea maybe arrested, detained or expelled.... Since 1998, four U.S citizens have been detained by North Korean authorities.

My tapes and films contain roads, highways, bridges, and railroad stations. I also recorded People's Army soldiers, hungry mothers and their small children, and peasants who look miserable. Can they escape the search?

I hear my heart jumping at my throat. Again, as at the beginning of our journey, all the passengers stand up to form a line in the aisle, and the search has already started at the other end of the train. This time, I am the last one of the long queue. The wait makes me even more nervous. All the doors and windows are closed and the train attendants, who were friendly and laughing with us moments ago, have already got off the train, watching us from outside the windows. I look at the young attendant, but he looks in another direction.

Last night at the hotel, I hid the tapes and notes in the inner pockets of a coat. But the soldier will feel them if I place the jacket in my bag. Then, I remember that the last time, the soldier did not search my body. I quickly take out the coat from the bag and put it on. The line moves forward. Those who pass the inspection are let go and group together, as ordered, in the center of the platform. I envy them for their newfound freedom, for that freedom becomes valuable only after I have lost it, even temporarily.

Passengers are released one after another. Finally, the soldier puts his white-gloved hands deep into my blue bag. It is almost empty; all the tomatoes and cucumbers are gone. He takes out a small box holding a couple of Korean dolls in colorful gowns. They are hand-carved and painted. The girl has a long oval face and a pair of big black eyes. Her red robe shines with tiny flowers. The man wears a sky blue gown with a red belt. I purchased them at the Friendship Store in Pyongyang. The store asked for 100 yuan, even though the tag labels showed 30 yuan. The clerk finally gave up and sold them to me at the tag price. Another woman was not this lucky. She wanted to buy a handmade silk purse. The tag price was 40 yuan, but she was charged 120 yuan. She could not believe that North Koreans are more money-driven than people in many capitalist countries.

The soldier puts down the dolls and picks up my scrapbook, which is empty. He focuses his attention totally on my belongings, but not on me. He must have also been tired after the hour-long search. The man straightens himself and orders me out of the train. Carrying my unzipped bag, I hurry to the door.

In the center of the platform, Little Wang has again arranged the small plastic stools in rows. No one knows when the train will come. Again, armed soldiers block us on all four sides, preventing any local person from approaching us. From the windows, I can see the silent eyes and bony faces inside the train station. Curious children with runny noses, dirty fingers in mouth, look at us from afar.

At long last, our train enters the station. In the "special express," the same ferocious-looking train attendant patrols the carriages and checks on the windows to make sure that they are all shut. Sitting in the sealed car, I feel like living in a cage. The search has ruined my mood. The others also wear long faces, sitting in complete silence. Outside, the now-familiar scene flashes by: mountains with bald spots, valleys decorated with numerous small patches growing thin crops, cottages on the verge of collapse, villages devoid of life, women crawling in the fields with small children on their backs and bigger ones at their sides.

Slowly, our train reaches the Yalu River Bridge. A little farther on is the international boundary. Along the Chinese side, flocks of ducks and geese swim merrily, stirring ripples around them. Tall factories line the riverbank, spewing forth smoke from their chimneys. The green mountains ahead are lush with trees, and flat fields grow a variety of healthy crops. Peasants work diligently in the well-watered paddies. I am excited to hear the chickens, cows, children, cars, and tractors in the near distance. In my ears, they are playing a symphony of vigor and life, in stark contrast to the dead quietness from which we have just emerged.

The train rumbles to the middle of the river. Suddenly, all the passengers start talking at once. The ferocious looking North Korean train attendant lowers his eyebrows and humbly retreats into a corner.

The Guangdong man sitting behind me, always silent during the entire trip, starts talking silly in his heavily accented Mandarin, "…no one knows how many women Chairman Mao had…He loved to have women around him but never truly loved them…. His taste of women is low…"

Others laugh as soon as his voice drops.

Ji'an Station, and the Chinese border guards in light green uniforms appear in sight. I like the casual look on their young faces. I take a deep breath of relief: "The dangerous trip is over!"

As BBC News reporter Richard Lister was leaving North Korea after his coverage of Ms. Albright's visit to the country, he used the word "liberated" to describe his feeling. "North Korea is a sad and broken place which won't easily be mended," he concluded.

PART II

Bloody Yanbian

13. Massive Flight

In front of me is the Tumen River, which runs through the city bearing its name. This channel divides China's Jilin Province and North Korea's Hamgyong Buk-do Prefecture. It passes through the sacred Changbai Mountains (Mt. Paektu), famous for their icy beauty and the "Heavenly Lake" at the summit.

The Yanbian region of China is known as the "Little South" because of its lush mountains, network of rivers, creeks, and irrigations, and rich paddy fields. About half the population, or two million people, are Korean Chinese, who started coming to this part of Northeast China at the end of the 17th century. After the famine of 1869 came another influx. Immigration was also common after the establishment of the Japanese puppet state Manchukuo in 1932.

Tumen does not look like a forbidden border city. The town appears friendly, open, and welcoming. I do not see armed border guards patrolling with threatening German shepherds. I do not see tall watchtowers or barbed wire barriers. Traditionally, there was no clear borderline between China and North Korea, and people of both sides visited each other freely. Locals had never heard of IDs, visas, passports, or checkpoints. During the three-year famine caused by Mao's Great Leap Forward movement, many Chinese crossed the Tumen River to escape hunger.

The Tumen River, narrow and shallow, flows leisurely into the Sea of Japan. There are many small islands in the middle of the stream. On China's side floats a red pavilion dock to which are tied many small sightseeing boats. A group of Korean-Chinese men wearing traditional-style straw hats sit around a stone table, playing chess with numerous bystanders cheering and jittering.

The Chinese side of the Tumen River, appearing peaceful, open and friendly.

North Korea's Namyong lies directly opposite to Tumen. The bright day yields a crystal-clear view. Security on the other side is tight. Along the dirt path by the river, two Korean guards are patrolling. They carry long shotguns nicknamed 3/8s, which the Japanese soldiers used during the Second World War. Their hats tilt on their heads and their army coats, greasy and dirty, hang over their narrow bodies. Their steps look heavy, unstable, and tired. My camcorder stubbornly follows them. But if I think that the soldiers are too weak to do their job, I am wrong. One of the men notices me. He stops to watch, appearing confused, not knowing what kind of equipment I hold. He hesitates and moves along, swinging only one of his arms high. But his vigilance and sense of duty do not permit him to dismiss me. A few steps on, he pauses again and turns towards me. He looks with a hand shading his eyes from the blinding sunlight. Suddenly he bursts out, yelling and waving his gun toward me in a threatening gesture.

Once dusk falls, the border becomes another world. During nights without the moon and stars, under the cover of darkness, desperate North Korean men, women, and even children wade through the shallow water. On the Korean side of the river, in the many mountain bunkers where eyes cannot see, hide North Korean border soldiers, ready to shoot any-

A group of Korean Chinese play cards on the stone table by the Tumen River in China.

one who attempts to escape the country. It is easy for the escapees to cross the narrow Tumen River in any season. During spring, they can swim across. During summer, they can wade across. During winter, they can walk across. The entire crossing takes only two or three minutes. Bribes also work. With 50 won in their pockets, the soldiers will let anyone pass through at night. If a great deal more is paid, the border guards will even allow passage during daytime, leaving their stations purposely for lunch.

Ever since the massive flight started years ago, the Tumen area has become an extremely sensitive border region. Officially, both countries prohibit photos and filming. But tipped by a local woman, I paid 20 yuan to the Chinese immigration officers stationed at the international bridge and was led to the top of the customs building overlooking Namyong. Like everywhere else I have seen in North Korea, the city is lifeless and in terrible condition. But for the starving North Koreans, this is a land of hope. Many would walk for days or even weeks from other cities to meet with their Chinese relatives at the Tumen International Bridge, hoping that their kin will bring them food. Maybe 50 kilograms of wheat, 80 kilograms of rice, 100 kilograms of corn, some winter clothes, other daily necessities such as cooking oil, sugar, salt, pills....[1] If their relatives did not get their letters and fail to show up, they are doomed, for they have no strength to walk all the way back home, and even if they did, basic

Thousands upon thousands of North Koreans, in all seasons, cross the narrow Tumen River to China to escape death at home.

problems would not be solved there: they can eat only one meal every few days. Then they think about their children: their stomachs bloated, arms hanging like twigs and eyes staring vacant. Their old parents come across their minds. Their mothers and grandmothers would die first, for the elderly women would save food for the young. In some places, it is hard to see adults above fifty years old and children under seven still alive. Corpses are left unburied in the streets of the rural areas or at home.

Schools have shut down. Tuberculosis, rickets, and pneumonia, all hunger-related diseases, strike hard. In August 1999, the Children's Fund of the United Nations found that about 80,000 North Korean children had died. And about 800,000 more were dying from malnutrition.

Some parents kill their children rather than see the little ones die slowly. Other families eat a last meal mixed with rat poison. At first, the government banned tombstones in the graveyards to hide the massive numbers of deaths. Later, it prohibited public funerals to keep the tragedies secret.

Everywhere, people swollen with edema can be seen. The desperate dig seeds in the fields owned by the collective communes. The government executes these "criminals." It also sends the families of those who have escaped to China to labor camps. Sometimes those who voice complaints have been burned to death.

The Tumen and Yalu rivers, to the miserable North Koreans, are the only routes leading to life. No one, no power in the world, can stop the exodus.

"How many North Koreans altogether have escaped to China?" I ask my taxi driver, a young Korean-Chinese man. Xiao Len scratches his head.

"A lot. Every village along the border has at least five or six. One time, I heard the Chinese border guards complain that on an average day, about 35 to 50 cross the Tumen River."

"Do you know any of them so that I can talk to them?"

He looks hesitant. "They don't like meeting strangers. You know our government is looking for them and sending them back."

"Why?" I am not only shocked but also angry.

"At first, our government agencies were very lenient to the escapees. Who doesn't have a human heart? Who is not sympathetic to the poor things? What's more, these folks are our relatives. We gave them food and places to live in and let them work at our homes and businesses. We paid them small cash, even though we are not rich, either. Then, more and more of them crossed the river because it is getting easier to leave ... if they can pay the border guards 500 won [$200]. Our side still kept one eye closed. But Kim Jong Il protested. He accused China of damaging the friendship between the two countries and demanded that it take action and send the 'national traitors' back."

Under pressure, the Chinese government has agreed to cooperate with Kim Jong Il. In accordance with a bilateral treaty between the two countries, China is obligated to catch and deport the escapees if the North Korean government demands it. China also has its own reasons for sending back the escapees. These people, who are willing to do anything with very little compensation, take jobs away from the local population. Unemployment is very serious in China's northeast region. Many state-owned enterprises in Yanbian Korean Autonomous Prefecture have failed and one in every two households has an unemployed worker.

Xiao Len continues, "With the influx of the North Korean escapees, the crime rate has risen dramatically. The homeless and moneyless people steal whenever and wherever they can, kidnapping travelers and robbing buses. Many, including hungry Korean border guards, also cross the Tumen River to rob and then return." To legitimize its sending back the North Koreans, the Chinese government refuses to recognize them as international refugees, but calls them 'illegal immigrants' instead.

It is gut-wrenching to think of the escapees sent back into the hands of the Kim Jong Il government.

"On the bridge over there"—the young man points to the Tumen

International Bridge only ten meters away — "the captives are handed over to the North Korean soldiers, who poke thick iron wires through their shoulders and link them in a string so that none can escape. Sometimes, the soldiers even put the wire through people's noses or ears," Xiao Len says, his voice rising.

"He is right!" A passerby agrees. This is an old man in Korean-style white attire. "The soldiers even do the same to children. Everyone in Tumen has seen the handover ceremony.

"In the past, the captives were killed instantly as national traitors. But in recent years, with so many people running away from the country, most are sent instead to labor camps." Volunteering what he knows, the old man officially joins us. "I have many relatives living there. If you want to know about North Korea, you should ask me, not him. He still smells his mother's milk, doesn't he?" the old man jokes.

"Those pitiful captives are put in tiny cells. You know, the winter here can get cold. It is hard to survive without heating in a room. But the North Korean camps have no heating even when the temperature drops to around -10 to -15°C. The inmates have no winter clothes or shoes. They are chained together and beaten with clubs. What is worse, they are given only thin corn soup. Some are so hungry that they even eat mud."

U.S. sources report that about 378,000 to 1.9 million people pass through the hundreds of detainment camps each year. Each camp can hold between 300 to 1,500 people.[2]

"My neighbor's North Korean wife was caught here in Tumen when she was shopping and was sent to a detention camp. But her Chinese husband borrowed several thousand yuan and paid someone in the camp who has a say, and the wife came back home with him."

"Their border guards love our products," Xiao Len continues, "Sometimes, if you give them things, they will let you pass the checkpoint on the international bridge. It is that easy."

As we talk, an old blue truck passes across the bridge, driving back to Namyong. On the streets of Tumen, as in Dandong, North Korean traders, who must come from pure proletarian families so they are immune to the influence of Chinese capitalism, drive Soviet-made trucks. They load whatever they can get — seeds, sacks of rice, wheat and corn, meat, clothes, cigarettes and other daily necessities. In exchange, they bring in brown feather fans, among other merchandise. These are unique fans. Larger feathers are arranged along the outside, with the smaller ones in the inner circle. In the center, two tiny birds stand facing each other. The handle is painted cheap purple, with "Pyongyang" written in gold. It is pinned against a repeatedly recycled paperboard and wrapped with low-quality plastic paper. This fan is the work of North Korean women and children, who gather the feathers one by one in the fields or by the roadsides.

In the stores near the Chinese immigration checkpoint on the International Bridge, badges of Kim Il Sung and Kim Jong Il are for sale at steep prices. The most expensive is the one with the heads of both father and son engraved on a flying red flag. Only ranking Korean officials can wear this type of badge. Ordinary North Koreans wear smaller ones with a single head of either Kim. The storeowners obtained the badges from North Korean children who swim across the river and sell the badges very cheaply in exchange for food.

All the stores sell North Korean money at a very low price, even though the official exchange rate is one Korean won to four Chinese yuan. The 100-won note shows the upper body of Kim Il Sung wearing suit and tie. On the 50-won note are a man in worker's overalls and a woman in hanbok, the traditional gown. The Juche Tower rises in the background. The 10-won note depicts a square-faced worker operating a machine. Behind him is the famous chollima, or "Thousand League Horse," which symbolizes the speed of North Korea's socialist transformation. All the stamps express similar themes, but with bolder colors. Workers and peasants stride forward, carrying high the Workers Party flags and holding sickles and hammers.

Other than the legal trade between the two sides, the storeowners tell me that many of the cheap goods on sale are smuggled by North Korean housewives. On their heads, they carry the merchandise, disguised as laundry, and wade into the Yalu or Tumen rivers. Normally, the Chinese buyers would approach the ladies on the Korean side of the rivers. But often, the two sides would do business just in the center of the rivers, which are only waist-deep. When the Chinese buyers receive the goods, they put the money in a sealed plastic bag and attach a piece of stone to it. Then they throw the bag to the bank. There, the North Korean housewives can safely pick up their payments. In case the soldiers want to intervene, the housewives would pound on their chests and pull their hair, shrieking in tears, "Kill Me! Kill Me! What is wrong with me meeting my relative in the River? I don't want to live. Shoot me! Shoot me!"[3] Their innocent cries make the confused soldiers feel guilty. Anyway, these are women, harmless housewives.

The deal done in the midstream eliminates bribing the border guards so both sides harvest bigger profits.

Quickly, this practice has developed into people trafficking. Human traders smuggle the North Koreans to China where they arrange meetings with

Chollima, "Thousand League Horse," statue in downtown Pyongyang suggests the speed of the socialist construction in North Korea. This image is on the 10-won note.

their South Korean relatives. The business, though risky, is lucrative. Human traders charge $50 to $100 or more to smuggle a person out of North Korea to China or return him to the North if he so wishes. The North Korean smugglers must not only maintain intimate relationships with the North Korean State Security Agency, People's Security Ministry officials, and border guards, but also with their Chinese counterparts.

When the border guards collect payments from the traffickers, they also hide the customers near the rivers. The smugglers look after the border troop's daily meals and often hold liquor parties. To win the border guards' trust, the human smugglers must act like their family members and must be loyal to their connected border soldiers. If unrelated guards catch

The Korean Chinese live a casual life in China's Yanbian Korean Autonomous Prefecture while their relatives across Tumen River try to flee death in North Korea.

them, they would rather die than tell the truth. Their sacrifices in turn deepen the relationship with their connections.[4]

Kim Jong Il is fully aware of the business, and has ordered the executions of scores of human traffickers in the border cities of Sinuiju and Hyesanjin in recent years. Because of his harsh crackdowns, it is very hard to find a human smuggler these days. But Kim Jong Il cannot completely uproot the cross-border smuggling unless the country's overall situation improves.

14. Cold Water Village

My taxi driver Xiao Len's home village is called Cold Water. It is a small mining community located ten kilometers from the city of Tumen. The young man says that at least five North Korean escapees are hiding there. Slowly we pass brick houses encircled with wattle fence, and the spacious backyards where noisy chickens, geese, and dogs scamper about. As we continue along the dirt road, I see a tall, slim woman walking ahead. She wears a red and green flowery shirt, the kind rural women in the northern provinces prefer. She opens her mouth slightly when she sees our car. Her bronze-colored face looks panicky.

"She is a North Korean woman. Escaped here a few years ago and married a widower who is twenty years her senior."

"How old is she?"

"In her early thirties."

The woman looks much older than her real age. Starvation and weariness must have aged her. Her cheekbones stand out below a pair of big black eyes. Her skin is coarse. Her eyes are sad, lacking the lively look in the eyes of other rural women. Years ago, the brave woman waded through the Tumen River to escape hunger, leaving her husband and two children behind in North Korea. Although she has a new family with a Korean Chinese man here in Cold Water, she still misses her first husband and sons dearly.

"Every morning, she would stand in front of her house, looking across the mountains and weeping. I saw her wiping tears away when hoeing in the fields, stopping from time to time to look in the direction of North Korea," Xiao Len says. "Her children live right behind the big mountains, but she can't see them. She doesn't know if they are still alive or not. It is really heart-wrenching to see her weep like that every day."

I poke my head out of the window, wanting to talk to her, but she quickly chooses another route, dust flying from under her hurrying feet.

"The North Korean escapees are afraid to see strangers and decline any interviews. If news leaks, they can be caught and sent back. Nowadays, the police are looking for them everywhere," Xiao Len explains.

Our car stops in front of a red-brick house with wide eaves and rising roof, typical Korean-style architecture. In Yanbian Korean Autonomous Prefecture, it is common to see such structures standing side-by-side with the flat-topped Chinese cottages. Behind the house, fields stretch far into the distance. There, a tiny couple in their seventies is busily engaged, weeding and separating seedlings.

"Uncle Choi, come here! You have a guest," Xiao Len shouts.

The old man raises his head. "Oh! Xiao Len," he utters in surprise and stands up. Rubbing his soil-stained hands on his pants, he walks out of the field.

"Uncle Choi, this is a lady from a big city. She wants to know about the North Koreans hiding in our Cold Water."

Uncle Choi is a Korean Chinese. He immigrated to China in the early twenties when only a child. His face, though browned from farming all his life, looks healthy. Underneath his gray cap, which matches the color of his pants, his two slim eyes shine with wisdom and caution. Smoothing his striped sweater, he invites us into the house.

Inside, a brick stove and a huge water jar buried halfway into the ground face the door. That is the kitchen. On its right side, a short staircase leads to the main room. There, a brick bed is connected to the stove in the kitchen so that when cooking, the heat can warm the bed.

Following Korean custom, I take off my shoes before entering the formal room. The peasant's life has changed tremendously during China's economic reforms. Modern appliances—television, digital clock, telephone and refrigerator—grace the spacious room. The bedding is quite fancy. A quilt in red satin embroidered with huge golden phoenixes has been folded into a square. The floor shines, dustless.

The Korean Chinese are a clean people and proud that most of their homes are tidier and neater than those of the Han Chinese. The Han majority, on the other hand, are known for being broad-minded and tolerant. For generations, the two races have coexisted peacefully and harmoniously in Yanbian Korean Autonomous Prefecture. Xiao Len, my taxi driver, says that in Cold Water, there have never been racial conflicts among the residents—half of them are Han Chinese and half Korean Chinese—even

In China's Yanbian Korean Autonomous Prefecture, a Korean-Chinese couple work very hard on their private land. With the privatization of Mao's people's communes in China, the motivated peasants are not only self-sufficient but also have surplus to sell for money.

though they wear different clothes, eat different food, and practice different customs.

Uncle Choi sits on the edge of the brick bed, his hands fidgeting on his lap. His weathered face shows a suppressed smile. He looks a little uneasy. There are no chairs in a Korean-style room, so Xiao Len and I sit on the floor with our legs under our hips.

"Uncle Choi, where is Park?" Xiao Len asks.

Park is Uncle Choi's North Korean relative who escaped to China only several months ago.

The old man shakes his head. "I am a Chinese Communist Party member. If the officials find out, I will be fined for harboring an escapee. God knows how much it will be for the punishment."

The old man continues, "Even for me to talk to you about the topic, you must obtain permission from the town Party secretary."

"Please, Uncle!" Xiao Len does not believe in the town Party secretary. The warm-hearted young man begs his next-door neighbor. "Why so afraid? Does she look like a bad person? Just tell the truth."

"The truth? But I can't just say things that come to my mind. Are you from Shanghai?" He asks me. "That is a big city. Here, we don't see many people from big cities. You have come a long way, so I don't want to disappoint you." The old man sighs a deep sigh, his eyes gloomy.

"Having lived in China for more than half a century, I already consider myself Chinese. But I cannot forget my hometown across the Tumen River. My relatives are still living there. We still hear from each other from time to time.

"I have to say that God is unfair to the Koreans. Too many people in the small peninsula, not enough arable land. All the plains are on the side of China, but all the rugged mountains and rocky hills are in Korea. Life has always been difficult and food always a problem. These years, things are getting from bad to worse there. Just take a look at their crops and ours. Theirs are thin and weak because they have no fertilizers to apply. Last year, their harvest produced little or no corn, while ours made more than we needed. Our warehouses are spilling with grain, and we have to build more storage places. People across the river are starving. In the fields, they dig up the seeds as food and eat up the young seedlings before they have a chance to yield crops. Look at their villages. They have no cows, pigs, donkeys, or mules. Even the ducks and geese swim on our side of the river.

"By nature, we Koreans are a happy people. Traditionally, we like singing in colorful clothes and dancing to the beat of long drums. But today, North Koreans have learned to keep their mouths shut. Those who complain will disappear the next day. There are many mysterious kidnappings in the country. So, people simply don't speak."

Annual reports by the U.S. State Department indicate that in 2002, North Korea held 200,000 political prisoners.[1] Whoever criticizes Kim Il Sung and Kim Jong Il is a political rival. A professor was sentenced to work as a laborer simply because he said in class that Kim Il Sung had received little formal education. Extrajudicial killings and disappearances also occur. Kim Il Sung once said, "factional elements have errors filled to the top of their heads, and must be isolated deep in the remote mountains." Following his words, the government took people who dared complain from their homes late at night and sent them directly to the camps in those isolated regions known as the "Restricted Areas." Prison conditions are harsh. Inmates are sentenced to death for such ill-defined "crimes" as "ideological divergence," "opposing socialism and revolution," "defection and attempted defection," "listening to foreign broadcasts," "writing reactionary letters," and "possessing reactionary printed matter."

The great famine that has lasted for a decade is still far from over. Uncle Choi claims that a few of his relatives are among the millions of North Koreans who have starved to death.

"In today's North Korea, grass roots, cabbage stalks, pine tree leaves, barks, even worms and insects have become many people's daily diet. My relatives also eat this kind of food. Some people boil the pine tree bark over and over again for its limited oil and protein. Then, they put in a few grains of rice or corn to make porridge. When children eat the mixture, they vomit and vomit until they have nothing to throw up. Infants who take it go blind. At the peak of hunger in 1997, the desperate ate fine dirt, which caused severe constipation. Countless people were bloated to death. Some survived by chewing dead bodies. Some ate their own infants. Others exchanged children with neighbors because they could not kill their own. Child murderers kidnapped children and sold their flesh, disguised as beef or lamb, in the black market at extravagant prices. In my brother's village, the government executed a couple. A woman recognized that the meat she bought from them in the black market was half of an infant's rear end. Then, the villagers found dozens of children's skeletons buried in their backyard.

"Cannibalism has occurred. It is not a rumor. When people have nothing to eat, they become crazy and turn on each other."

Uncle Choi sighed, his eyes red. Then he added, "Both physically and spiritually hungry people turn to religion, but they are deemed insane if they believe in God. If you pray and someone hears your prayer, you are doomed. Religious prisoners are considered the most dangerous and treated more harshly even than political offenders. They are given almost nothing to eat, beaten severely, often left dying in the tiny cell."

Annual reports by the U.S. State Department in 2002 indicate that "members of underground churches have been killed because of their religious beliefs and suspected contacts with overseas evangelical groups operating across the Chinese border...."

As if having shifted a heavy burden off his back, Uncle Choi stands up. His restless hands are now relaxed.

"Go around the village, and you may meet with a few of the escapees hiding here. They take refuge in every village along the border. We are their relatives. If we don't help them, who will? During our great famine in the sixties, many of us crossed the Tumen River to find food there. North Korea then was heaven to us, even richer than South Korea. Now, the unlucky ones have to run back.

Xiao Len drives slowly. He is proud of his car, which he purchased after having sold two cows that he had raised for years. News spreads fast in this small mining community. Local people still do not see many cars in the border village. Children come out of their houses to watch the automobile.

A man and a woman stand by the roadside in front of a lush vegetable garden. The young woman, with smiling eyes and full lips, looks very pretty.

"Here is another North Korean woman. The couple lives at the east end of the village. The Korean-Chinese man paid 2,000 yuan and bought her as his wife. A rich businessman in downtown lent the husband the money and promised to cancel half or all of the debt if he could sleep with the pretty North Korean woman. We often see the businessman leaving the couple's house in the morning in a car. The wife seldom comes out of her house. Once she told her neighbor that she had become a sex slave of two men. She said that her husband chained her hand to a table leg. He set her free only after she told him in tears that she could not run anywhere because she cannot speak Chinese, does not have any money, and has no relatives or friends to help her in strange towns and cities. She has no place to go."

Explaining, Xiao Len stops the car beside them. The woman looks horrified, trying to hide behind her husband. The man explodes in anger. His eyes wide open, he waves his fist, threatening to beat us.

"Don't worry. He's just afraid that his wife will be arrested and sent back," Xiao Len says, "I have heard many tragic stories. Some couples like them have been married for years. But the North Korean mothers and their children still can't obtain legal status. The women can't work and the children can't go to school. And these days, the situation is getting worse. The police are hunting from door to door, deporting those who have no IDs. All Chinese citizens have picture Ids, so those who don't are obviously escapees."

In June 2001, after a family of seven North Koreans defected, escorted into the offices of the U.N. High Commissioner for Refugees (UNHCR) in Beijing by a freelance Japanese journalist, the Chinese government, fearing similar incidents, began deporting more escapees. Police go to people's homes, looking especially for North Koreans who have lived in China for more than five years, and fine the Korean-Chinese families who have helped their relatives.

While China's northern cities usually have a rich variety of nightlife, in border cities such as Yanji, the capital of the Yanbian Korean Autonomous Prefecture, stores close early and the streets are deserted. In downtown Yanji, I happen to witness a government crackdown. In one of the few night market areas, teams of policemen appear out of nowhere. They stop in front of stores, and yell at the workers, demanding IDs and questioning employees. Some frightened workers attempt to hide, others try to run away. The police threaten to tear down the stands and confiscate all merchandise if the workers fail to show their IDs. And they have got the right targets. Many simply cannot produce IDs because they are North Koreans hired by the local Korean Chinese. A woman being taken away by the police cries frantically to a horror-stricken, pale-faced child. Then the youngster is taken away also.

The North Korean escapees who are hired to watch over shops are considered lucky. Most others work on farms or in mines, or just hide in the mountains. In 2001, the Chinese government sent back, on average, two dozen escapees, adults and children alike, to North Korea every day.[2]

According to the office of the United Nations High Commissioner of Refugees, there are about twenty million refugees throughout the world today. Under international human rights regulations, the country of first refuge is required to accept them temporarily until they can return or find a new home in some other country.[3]

Amnesty International protests the Chinese government's sending back the North Korean escapees. In a letter to President Jiang Zemin in July 2001, the organization said, "Those detained in the crackdown are being denied access to any refugee determination procedure and pushed back over the border to meet an uncertain fate. This could include imprisonment, torture and in some cases summary execution or death in detention from starvation and disease."

On March 14, 2002, twenty-five North Koreans, including eleven aged 10 to 19, disguised as tourists, rushed through the open gates of the Spanish Embassy Compound in Beijing. The six families and two orphaned girls threatened to commit suicide if sent back to North Korea:

"We are now at the point of such desperation and live in such fear of persecution within North Korea that we have come to the decision to risk our lives for freedom rather than passively await our doom. Some of us carry poison on our person to commit suicide if the Chinese authorities should choose once again to send us back to North Korea."[4]

Urged to "solve the issue in accordance with humanitarian concerns," Chinese Premier Zhu Rongji agreed to send the escapees to the Philippines.[5]

But a new roundup of the North Korean escapees followed and more escapees are deported across the border every day. In the tears and cries of the hopeless people, Yanbian turns bloodier.

15. The Dangerous Life of the Escapee

At Uncle Choi's house in Cold Water, I meet Park, a thirty-year-old North Korean man. He sits on the brick bed, wearing a fashionable yellow and black sweatshirt and a pair of khakis, which he obviously bought from one of the countless clothing stores in the city of Tumen. The man is bony and dark skinned with a thin, long neck. His Adam's apple moves up and down conspicuously. Two deep wrinkles cut through his forehead. This rugged face belongs to a young Korean man who should be as strong as a tiger, but he is silent, withdrawn.

Although the back windows face a vast piece of farmland and rippling mountains, Uncle Choi still closes the windows and draws the curtains. The room is dim. With Uncle Choi sitting at his side as his interpreter, Park begins his story.

"I lived with my parents in Hamgyong-namdo Province located in the northern region. Although both my parents and I were workers, we remained at the bottom of North Korea's society for all our lives. The Korean Workers Party doesn't trust us because we have relatives living in China." Park points to Uncle Choi, who is his father's elder brother.

"My father could never join the Korean Workers Party. But I wanted to change my fate. I planned on entering the People's Army, the first step in becoming a Party member. But my father, who hated the Army, bribed the military doctor, who failed my physical examination. That ended my dream once and for all.

"For us, living in the northern region, the famine started as early as

127

in 1993, one year before the death of Kim Il Sung. At first we received less than five kilograms of rice every month. Then heavy floods drowned the factories and mines. Electricity was cut off. Working in the darkness, we could not see one another, and many were killed in accidents. Soon, all food supplies stopped. Getting things to eat became our daily priority. As we received only a portion of our salaries, and sometimes no money at all, we couldn't afford food in the black market. We began stealing, anything from coal and lumber in the factories to chickens and cows in the communes. Some of my co-workers were caught and executed instantly. In the winter, filthy homeless people crowded the waiting rooms of the nearby train station. They lost their homes because they had sold them for food. In fact, people sold all their belongings for food. But they were still hungry. Dead bodies piled up behind the train station. Pretty much everywhere you went, you saw people alive one minute ago dropping dead the next.

"When we sold out everything in our home, I began traveling all over the country hunting for food. Most often, I went to the border. In the past, no one wanted to live in those mountainous regions near China, but now they are the most popular because abundant food supplies infiltrated from China sell in both black and open markets there.

"From 1993 to 1998, I walked throughout the villages along the border searching for food and learned how to deal with the secret police checkpoint, the most dangerous threat to ordinary people like me. Despite my desperate efforts, tragedy still struck my family. In the spring of 1997, when I carried a bag of rice and happily returned home, what I saw were the bodies of my parents—they had starved to death on their beds. Hugging their decomposed bodies, I began to cry. I blamed myself for not being a good son. What if I had returned home earlier? I could have saved their lives. Then, I imagined my own skeleton lying on the bed. The Party's call to the people to start the "Bitter Long March" and "Safeguard the Top Revolutionary Leader" suddenly became empty and meaningless.

"I heard myself shouting, 'Kim Jong Il! Kim Jong Il! What a monster you are!'

"But I was horrified to find myself repeatedly condemning our dear leader. This was the first time that I had cursed him since I was born. It was too dangerous. Everyone in North Korea knows what will await me if I doubted Kim Il Sung or Kim Jong Il. Ever since that moment, I no longer felt safe living in North Korea. I decided to escape to China and never come back. I went to the grave of my parents to say good bye. I journeyed to the border. At midnight, I plunged into the Yalu River.

"First, I went to China's Jilin Province, though not here in Tumen. I worked in a lumber plant. There, I met Mr. Jung, a Korean Japanese. He told me that the Koreans in Japan are against Kim Jong Il's regime. He said that North Korea should have a democratic government. I was terrified. However, when I thought about the deaths of my parents and my tragic flight from North Korea, I cried bitterly like a little boy. I thought long and hard and decided that I should do something for my own people. I wanted to carry Jung's mini-camera and sneak back across the Yalu River to take pictures of the tragic situation in North Korea. I knew how to elude the secret police stations and how to bribe the officials. In case I was arrested, I also knew how to run away. At worst, I would bite off my tongue to keep the secret.

"Jung and I named the action 'China — Schlinder Battle.'

"I opened many small holes in my bag so I could take pictures while walking without causing suspicion. I also brought with me many packs of cigarettes, which are excellent bribes, along with Korean and foreign money. Chinese yuan can be used along the border, but in the interior, I must change it into won, the North Korean currency.

"I would first go to the central regions. I had friends living there. Although I wanted very much to go back to my hometown in the north, I decided not to. Since I had been missing for a long time, the authorities, who strictly controlled the whereabouts of persons, would recognize me.

"The next night, I climbed down a cliff of 20 meters near the Yalu River, and waited for the signal: match lights to shine on the other side. In about two hours, a light flickered two times from across the River. It was the go-ahead sign. Immediately, I waded through the water. The River was shallow. Even the deepest place reached only to my stomach. In just a few minutes, I arrived at the other side, and the border guard whom I had already bribed met me at the bank. The North Korean border guards like the returnees from China, calling them "fat ducks," for they have money and good cigarettes. The young border guard led me over the hills to avoid the secret police. After hours of walking, I finally saw a farmhouse. The owner let me in, gave me some corn to eat and put me in a window-less storage room. I hid there for days.

"In every village, there is a system known as the 'People's Class,' which uses villagers to watch their neighbors and report strangers to the author-ities. Any outsider who wants to spend a night in the village must regis-ter with the system, which is extremely strict along the borders. Militias and soldiers patrol all day and night, searching every household. They open trunks and suitcases and look under beds. Because I couldn't show my real ID, I ran a great risk staying long in the village.

"I sneaked into the nearby train station. After I paid the conductor 800 Chinese yuan, he asked me to sit next to him so as to evade the policemen's routine search of the passengers at every stop. But when the train arrived at a small station, a policeman suddenly appeared in the conductor's room. He looked at me up and down.

"'Hey, who are you? Show me your ID,' he yelled.

"My spine turned stiff.

"'You don't look like a conductor. What are you doing here?'

"'I don't have an ID,' I shouted at the policeman while quickly opening the door and jumping out of the train.

"I ran madly ahead until I was sure that no one was chasing me. I was so hungry that I could not walk any longer. I had had nothing to eat for days. Although I had money in my pocket, I could find no restaurants or food stands. I struggled for another kilometer before I came into a black market and purchased a baked potato there. Having filled my stomach, I stood by the roadside, trying to stop a truck that would take me to the city of Manpu. I waved cigarettes to lure passing drivers to stop. I bargained with them. Finally I reached an agreement with an old driver: I would pay him a pack of Chinese Yunnan cigarettes in exchange for a ride. The truck carried no goods, but was filled with hitchhikers in foul clothes.

"As we talked, a man climbed onto the truck from the other side. The driver yelled at him, 'Pay at least for the oil or get off. Without money, I can't buy oil, OK?' "The man begged, 'Dear old uncle, I have walked for days and haven't eaten anything yet. Look at my legs. They are shaking from hunger. Where can I get the money to pay for the gas? Please, be merciful. Otherwise ...' he wiped his wet eyes.

"The driver turned to me, took the pack of cigarettes and put it in his pocket so he could sell it later at a steep price in the black market. The truck was so crowded that I almost sat on people's heads and shoulders. Needless to say, the trip was exhausting but what made it unforgettable was a tragedy that I witnessed.

"When the truck driver stopped in a town to take a short break, a policeman approached the young woman next to me, who held a stuffed bag tightly in her arms.

"'Get off the truck,' the policeman yelled and grabbed the bag from her.

"The angry woman stood up abruptly. She raised one of her hands to touch the high-voltage wire above her head while grasping the policeman's arm with the other. The powerful electricity threw the two into midair, their bodies twisting and limbs tangling together. Tiny potatoes rolled out of the woman's cloth bag. Hungry people rushed to them. I covered my face and forgot that I should take pictures. For the rest of the trip, the woman's hopeless eyes kept flashing in my mind. But I did not cry, for I had no tears. I could no longer feel fear or sorrow; all my senses had become dull.

"'Am I still a human being?' I asked myself repeatedly.

"At night, I got off the truck. I walked for a kilometer and knocked on the door of a lonely house by the roadside. I handed 10 won to the man who opened the door. He took the money but said nothing. The silence was a signal that he agreed to let me spend a night in his home. It was a shabby house. The unpainted walls looked ready to cave in. Mud was exposed from the big cracks. There was no furniture, actually nothing in the room except two pots on the stove. One was iron and the other clay. No lights. The room was dimly lit by the burning stove. The wife was sitting behind it. Even in the darkness, I could see her bright eyes. She was otherwise a beautiful woman, but hunger had reduced her to a walking skeleton. She held a little boy. The child's face was dirty. His thin body was trembling in his mother's arms. I paid them 20 won. The woman carefully put some corn powder into the boiling water. The porridge was tasteless, but at least it was pure, without grass roots and tree bark. It was the best they could entertain me with. Each of us holding a spoon, we sat around the clay pot and ate from it. They had no bowls in the house. The woman said that they had sold everything for food. With the 20 won I paid them, she would buy the little boy a piece of bread in the black market. She bowed to me several times. I looked at her but kept on thinking about the young woman holding tightly to her bag of potatoes.

"My camera has loyally recorded the miserable lives of the North Koreans. Here I am now hiding at my uncle's home. I wish that I could live in Cold Water for the rest of my life, but ... I will have to take another risky journey. This time, I will go to South Korea and I will get there."

16. Young Victims

Cold Water is just one of the many densely populated villages along China's border that shield countless North Korean escapees such as Park.

On the other side of the Tumen River, Workers Party propaganda tries to convince people that South Korea is a colony of the United States of America and beggars wander the streets. Life in North Korea is also better off than in China, which suffers from epidemics, famine and endless political struggles such as the Great Cultural Revolution. However, the common people are shocked at what they see once they cross the border.

"Along the main road, people stand out on their front steps, talking and laughing. The streets are brightly lit, neon signs glowing. Across the River, on the Korean bank, everything is still, enveloped in darkness."[1]

The Chinese in Yanbian entertain the Korean escapees with not only plenty of rice, but also abundant meat and good wine. As one escapee put it, "I felt as if I'd been invited to a feast for Party cadres. In North Korea, alcohol is very expensive. For a bottle, it costs 10 won ($5), 1/10 of a worker's salary. White wine is even more costly, 60 won ($30) for a bottle. Here in China, white wine is a normal dinner accompaniment. We can have it at every meal. Indeed, China is paradise... The River separates two worlds. In North Korea, citizens there feel they're under constant surveillance. The monitoring is systematic — when it's not your ID card they ask for, then it's your traveling papers...."[2]

"Our first border crossing is a grammar school degree, the second time we visit China is a high school diploma, and the third and fourth trips are our college and graduate degrees in reality. The North Korean government has been lying to us all these years."

When these "graduate students" and frequent border transgressors return to their home villages in North Korea, they tell their families and friends about China. This in turn causes more people to run away from North Korea, including many hungry children.

According to the United Nations, the year 2001 continued to see nationwide food crisis in North Korea after a poor fall harvest and the worst winter in fifty years. Serious fertilizer shortages, long-lasting natural disasters, limited cultivatable land and a short growing season have reduced staple grain output to 1.9 million tons.[3] The harvest meets less than the minimum food requirements. Most of the eight million North Korean children are in aid programs. But under the "no access, no aid" policy of the regime, about 20 percent of them, living in areas where the government allows no access to aid, are still starving.[4]

Therefore, getting food to eat is a daily goal in those deprived regions. Because of malnutrition, the underdeveloped children look smaller than their real age. Some are half-blind, crippled and suffer from various diseases. But their adventurous stories are equally compelling.

Before they fled to China, many North Korean girls had survived by selling blood or stealing corn from the grain train from Dandong, China. An eyewitness describes the following scene that happened along the railway:

"One night, I put on my shabby coat, carried a lamp and went to the train station. It was around 2 a.m. The grain train had already arrived. Five armed security officers watched the twelve cars. Then, in the split of a second, hundreds of thieves out of nowhere assaulted the cars. Strangely, at the moment, the armed officers were nowhere to be seen. The thieves crawled under the cars and broke open the bottom with tools. They filled their bags with the flowing grains. I was surprised to see that most of the robbers were girls. Their faces looked determined as if they were fighting on a battlefield. They clearly knew the danger because armed security officers could appear at any time and shoot them. But they were not afraid. If they missed this train, they did not know when the next grain train would come. Then, they would all starve to death."[5]

One teenage boy, Sung, had planned his escape to China for years. He was a good student at school and liked to read. But pupils dropped out of school one after another and finally the school closed. Sung's family lived on weed gruel, and their bodies and feet swelled up. Soon, Sung's younger brother died, followed by his grandmother. The family was so poor that they could not even afford a coffin. Sung's parents wrapped the old lady with a piece of white cloth, which was her bridal gift. Sung's father, who was a miner, left home to find food, never coming back. Sung's mother walked miles and miles looking for her husband. She never made it back, either. The young boy began living in the marketplace.

Sung recalls, "There were many children like me begging for food. The adults at the marketplace beat us if they caught us stealing. They kicked us until we bled. They stomped on our hands, but we still held fast to the food we stole. To get a few bites to eat, we did heavy labor for them. We gathered rocks in the mountains and brought them to the market and piled them up. We dug dirt and carried big buckets of water. But we never got enough to eat. Some children were so hungry that they would pick undigested corn from human waste or eat earthworms. At night, we would sleep on the cold ground, using a rock as a pillow and putting a few of the mats over our bodies as quilts.

"Then we heard about China: a rich country not far away. I decided to give it a shot. It would be better to die on the way to China than starving to death here. With some others, we climbed over mountains and forded streams before we arrived at the Tumen River. Many adults and children had already gathered at the bank, waiting for an opportunity. On a night without the moon and stars, we jumped into the river. The water reached my chest and choked me, but I kept on moving my legs and arms. The bright lights in the Chinese towns shone like beacons, opening up my escape path, and directing me to a land of hope.

"As soon as I crossed the river and my feet touched the ground, I broke into a run. At dawn, I was so excited to see the luxuriant fields, modern highways, and bustling villages. We, a group of starving children in rags, knocked on the door of a farmhouse and asked for food. People here in Yanbian are kind. They not only spoke our language but also dressed us, washed our faces, cleaned our dirty hair, and gave us lots to eat. That's how we live, from house to house. If we were still in North Korea, we would've died from hunger. A good thing about Yanbian is the food. In the market, we see lots of food that we have never seen before: creamy cakes, egg cookies, sweet pork and all kinds of beans, yellow, red, and green.... I like beans. It is marvelous that they also have kimchee here, our famous hot pickles. Yianbian people are our people. I feel at home with them. Buses and cars run well on the roads and all children can go to school even if they live in remote countryside. I wish that I could go to school, too. If not for the famine, the school would be open in my home country, and I would be in fifth grade. I really wish that my parents could live to see me so happy and feel satisfied."

However, China is not exactly paradise for the North Korean children. The life they face in Yanbian is also dangerous. Since they cannot speak Chinese, they become easy targets of gangsters, who beat and rob them, and force girls as young as 15 into prostitution. The girls sell their young bodies in the salons, bars and nightclubs all over Northeast China, in big cities and small towns alike. In one of the numerous nightclubs in Tumen, I see them walking around wearing translucent black gowns and high-heeled red leather shoes, soliciting the customers in broken Chinese, "Twenty yuan, Sir, if you like me." Desire for living wipes away their shyness at this tender age. Their heavily painted red lips half open, their lovely complexion appears snow-white against the colorful neon light flickering in the bar filled with fast music.

Traders in human beings also sell the North Korean girls as brides to the vast rural areas all over China. But even marriage to a Chinese citizen guarantees no protection from deportation. Unable to communicate with the Chinese, North Korean children can go nowhere. As illegal immigrants now and forever, they cannot attend school or enjoy any other benefits such as health and housing. In the city of Yanji, only 33 kilometers away from the border, I see small North Korean children begging for money in the markets. People throw pennies into the tin cans placed in front of them. In a street corner, a group of boys separate trash for recycling. No city dwellers would want to do this kind of work, although it does pay better than a formal factory job.

The homeless North Korean children live from hand to mouth, sometimes sleeping in cardboard boxes for the night. All the time, they have to be watchful, because the policemen are also after them, to capture and deport them.

Once caught and sent back to North Korea, the children are often jailed in a room so tightly packed that they cannot all sit at once, let alone sleep. Their persecutors ask them repeatedly the same three questions:

Do you go to China frequently?

Where do you go in China?

Above all, have you met South Koreans? Christians? Foreigners?

Two boys tell of their horrible experience being sent back to the North Korean camps.

"We lived in China's Hope County in Jilin Province and repaired roads for a month. We earned 500 yuan. We have never had so much money in our lives. We are good sons. When we had a little money, we thought about our starving parents and siblings back at home so we tried to sneak back to North Korea but got caught crossing the Tumen River. The guards confiscated all our money and put us into the Chongin provincial concentration camp jammed with "ideological offenders" who dared to question the correctness of Kim Il Sung's Juche theory. We were forced to repair roads and had to run while carrying the heavy loads of dirt and rocks.

"Having to work all day on food made from ground shells, cabbage roots mixed with corn flour, many people, old and young, collapsed. During our six months' stay there, among the 350 prisoners, 10 or more committed suicide and another 10 died from beatings. We don't know how many died from hunger."

The two boys were so hungry and so tired that they tried to kill themselves by eating nails, but they were caught and underwent forced surgery. After they were out of danger, the guards beat them, asking them if they had listened to South Korean broadcasts and met with South Koreans during their stay in China.

Although crippled from the severe beatings, the boys vowed to escape to China again. Unlike many other people who had never been to China and did not know anything about the outside world, the two boys had already experienced life across the Tumen River. They longed for that place day and night. Immediately after they were released, they dragged themselves to the border. It was hope that had sustained them: they wanted to live like human beings even for a day and see the real world before they died.[6]

At the beginning of 1999, Kim Jong Il tried again to stop the frenzied massive flight to China by issuing a new order: the escapees, regardless of their age, will receive five years in prison, and their families will be sent to the newly built provincial concentration camp in North Hamgyong province. There, the escapees and their families will do forced labor.

"If you are sent there, don't expect to get out alive," the escapees say, "there is no such thing as a family life. Men and women, mothers and children, live separately. The authorities say the sentence is only for five years, but the working and living conditions are so harsh that few can survive at the end."

Kang Chol Hwan, now living in South Korea, describes the fate of the North Korean youngsters: "Haggard children wander about with infected skin.... As soon as the first cold spells hit, they die of typhoid fever or cholera. Families are being torn apart. Parents frequently abandon their youngest children in the hope that one better off might find them and give them a home...."[7]

Kang Hyeok, a North Korean college student, says, "Young lives are lost to honor the slogan 'We will do whatever the Party asks us to do.' But where is our human dignity when mothers eat their sons, when students are dying in their classrooms? I cannot find human value anywhere in North Korea. It is a large prison surrounded by invisible steel bars. A hell on earth indeed."[8]

17. North Korea's Auschwitz

Lee Min-bok is a former researcher at the North Korean Science Academy. After years of research, he concluded that private farming in North Korea could produce three times more food than the collectives. Witnessing his countrymen dying from starvation, he wrote to the government, urging it to follow the China model and adopt a private farming system:

> Food shortage originates from the collective agricultural system, which gives farmers nothing of their product, no matter how hard they work all year round. China and Vietnam have recognized the problem, and transformed the system to that of private farming. They have achieved great success. Today, any North Korean who has the luck to look around China's villages would be surprised by the prosperity the Chinese peasants enjoy today.

He fled to China to avoid persecution for writing the letter, but was caught and sent back to North Korea.

Life at the concentration camps was harsh, Lee remembers. Camp officials told the inmates openly that in the camps, they should expect no humane treatment. The guards called them not by their names but by their prisoner numbers. Whenever the guards appeared, the inmates were forced to sit down, drop their heads, and act like slaves. No one could talk, laugh, stand, or lie down. No one could use the toilet without approval. The worst physical punishment was to sit for hours on the floor with one's legs under one's hips. The torture went on for about ten days. Each day all the inmates ate was a handful of boiled corn and a bowl of salty water. They were so hungry that they would often hallucinate about food, seeing a plateful of baked beef and a big bowl of white, oily rice mixed with beans, which are hardly seen in the market. Finally, physical torture and hunger turned them into a bag of bones. Many suffered from night blindness, pellagra, and scurvy caused by malnutrition.

They had no towels, no soap, no bath, no clean clothes, no toothbrushes, or toothpaste, not even toilet paper. The inmates had to share a piece of cloth and wash it afterwards. The toilet stool in the cell was also used as a basin to wash hands and face. Cockroaches infested the filthy cell. Lice crawled on the bodies and in the hair. Camp authorities took away even zippers, buttons and rubber bands from the clothes, so committing suicide was almost impossible for the miserable inmates, who would rather die than live.

In two weeks preliminary interrogations began. The inmates carried no handcuffs because everybody — guards, interrogators, and even the prisoners themselves — knew they were so weak that they could neither escape nor pose any threat.

The camp authorities also used inmates against each other. One day, Lee recalls, the guards provoked cellmates to beat to death Kim Jae-cheol, a thirty-two-year-old man from Yanggang-do Province, for complaining that he was so hungry eating only 100 grams (2.4 ounces) of food a day that he was losing his eyesight.

Lee estimates that about 20 to 30 percent of the prisoners died from hunger or hunger-related diseases in his camp.

The personal tragedy of Baek Iyong is no less shocking. Although Baek Iyong worked as Kim Jong Il's personal bodyguard, he secretly listened to the South Korean-run Korean Broadcasting Station and learned the truth about North Korea's economic crisis. In 1994, he defected to China. In Yanji, the capital city of the Yanbian Korean Autonomous Prefecture, he met with a South Korean diplomat, who was actually a North Korean agent in disguise. The agent won Lee's trust by offering him a pack of South Korean cigarettes. He told Baek Iyong that as a condition of going to South Korea, he must write a brief statement and read it in front of the journalists. In his statement, Baek Iyong disclosed secrets about Kim Jong Il's daily routine, such as when and where he would take a walk, where his office was located, its layout, and where his summer homes were. With such evidence, a group of North Korean agents abducted Baek Iyong to the North Korean embassy in Beijing. There, they injected him with anesthetics and morphine and put him on the Beijing-Pyongyang airplane.

In North Korea, Baek Iyong entered the No. 14 political prison, near Pyongyang, which contained about 15,000 political prisoners, including children.

Baek Iyong recalls that the prison authorities put a wooden stick with sharp edges behind his knees to force him to kneel. They kicked him with their heavy boots. They hung him by his hands so that he had to stand on his toes. At night, the guards filled his cell with water, making sure he was soaked in from his waist down. Standing in water for hours at a time, Baek Iyong's body swelled and his ankles and legs ached. When he could not stand up and fell, the guards beat him until he stood up again.

Baek Iyong's fate, compared to Kim Chul-min, was lucky. Chul-min, an inmate in the same camp, was ordered to drive trolleys and transport coal. There was a chestnut tree near the tracks. In autumn, the ripe chestnuts fell, covering the ground. For a hungry man, it was almost impossible to resist the temptation to pick up the nuts. Chul-min struggled not to look at the food. However, hunger finally conquered fear. One day, Chul-min got off his trolley and collected a handful of nuts, which he caressed gently and cleaned them with his sleeves. He had been so numbed by starvation and so overjoyed by having the nuts that he forgot the danger.

Before he had the chance to eat any of the nuts, the prison guards pushed him to the ground and kicked his head with their heavy boots. Blood streamed out of his nose and mouth. Then, the guards fastened one of Chul-min's legs to the trolley and drove the vehicle at top speed, dragging the poor man to his death.

Watching Chul-min's disintegrated body, other prisoners stood motionless in fear and anger. No one even looked at Chul-min's chestnuts scattering under their feet.

The fate of women was even more tragic in Camp No. 14. There was an executive suite for visiting officials from Pyongyang. When they came for inspection, attractive female prisoners from 21 to 25 were brought in to serve. Afterwards, they were blamed for trying to escape from the camp. They never returned to their cells. No one knew their whereabouts. Some speculated that they were secretly murdered to cover the truth. The practice was repeated whenever an official from Pyongyang came for a visit.

The political prisoners were also used as guinea pigs for testing chemical warfare weapons.

Within the camps, death lurked in every corner at any time.

Kang Chol Hwan, the defected North Korean writer, can never forget the public execution of a "traitor" that he witnessed in Yodok Camp. He writes, "It must have been ages since the condemned man had last eaten. All skin and bones…, [he] seemed no longer a member of the family of man. It would be easy to mistake him as an animal, with his wild hair, his bruises, his crusts of dried blood, his bulging eyes. Then, I suddenly noticed his mouth. So that's how they shut him up. They had stuffed it full of rocks."[1]

When a second "traitor" who somehow did not have enough rocks in his mouth began protesting his innocence and cursing that Kim Il Sung was "a little dog," a guard picked up a big rock and pushed it into his mouth, knocking out his teeth and bloodying his face.

Sex is banned among the inmates because the government believes that not only all the "criminals" but also their "next generation of counterrevolutionaries" should also perish in North Korea. If a man and woman violate the rules, authorities send the man to a sweatbox and humiliate the woman in a public meeting. There she will have to tell the details such as how she makes love and how her lover responds. One witness saw a woman bound to a tree with a breast cut off. A guard finally killed her by putting a spade handle into her vagina.

K Hyeok is a student from Susan College in Hamgyong-namdo.

Starting in 1993, the college students had had a ration of corn meal of only 120 grams (2.6 ounces) a day. Many of them suffered from serious malnutrition and were forced to quit school. Professors were too hungry to lecture. In winter, there was no heat in the dormitory. The students went to bed wearing winter clothes and thick socks, wrapping themselves with dirty blankets and embracing each other for warmth.

Yet the college still required the students to bring nails, light bulbs, and wallpaper to decorate the dormitory. The students used their food money to purchase these things in the black market. Starvation became worse in 1996 and the students could only eat soup of arrowroots mixed with corn flour. The students went to class but could not learn. All they thought was one thing, "Is there anything I can eat today? Where can I get it?" It was useless to think about food, but the starving students could not help it.

K Hyeok escaped to China in 2000 but was soon captured and sent back to his fatherland. He says that during the preliminary investigation, the guards ordered him to bend his back like a camel with his head on the ground. Then, they beat him with square bars, calling this the "camel torture."

"Have you met a South Korean in China?"

K Hyeok said no and the guards hit him again. Beatings continued day after day. The young man would tremble all over whenever he heard his own handcuff chains rattling when he was taken to the torture cell. K Hyeok felt the worst two or three minutes before the torture. But once it started, he was not scared. He did not feel much pain either, because his mind had become numb.

K Hyeok was also forced to watch a massacre of his cellmates whose crime had been to go to the South Korean Consulate General in Beijing to seek help during their exile in China. The South Koreans rejected their requests, and North Korean special agents later arrested them and brought them back. Having contact with South Korean people in China is regarded as treason, a high crime punishable by death.

"One morning, twenty-seven of us were put on a truck," K Hyeok recalls. "The truck ran along a steep mountain road and finally stopped in a valley. Three new pits seemed to open their mouths wide towards us. The bloodthirsty executioners were wearing black glasses and white gloves. Their guns shone on their shoulders. Then one of them shouted to us, 'If you are called, come forward!'

"Three men were ordered to stand with their backs toward a rock wall. Gunshots struck the first man's skull. I smelled the blood first before I heard the sound. The bullets passed through the man's chest and forehead. He leaned forward, his body shaking all over.

"The second man received one shot in the chest and another in the belly. He gripped his belly and stepped back. Then he raised his head, staring at his killer, clenching his teeth before collapsing to the snow-covered ground. Blood flowed, reddening the snow around him.

"The third man had already lost his senses. The executor approached him, smiling. He held his pistol against the man's head and pulled the trigger. Then, he fired randomly on the struggling man. Whenever a bullet penetrated into the body, I saw clearly that the flesh was trembling."

Having taught K Hyeok a lesson, the prison authorities transferred the college student to the Hyaeryeong Safety Bureau prison, which held countless border transgressors. It was early April. Through the bars of the cell windows, K Hyeok could see the apricot trees sprouting forth new buds. Swallows sang to him. Spring was coming. But it was dark and cold inside the prison.

Ash-faced inmates were groaning next to him. Every day, dead bodies were taken out of the tiny cells. K Hyeok missed his fiancée badly. Images of her kept flashing in front of his eyes. He could not forget the day, when they had been jailed in the same prison, that she had been ordered to clean the corridors. When the guards did not look, she slipped K Hyoek a piece of dried bread soiled with dust. He had no idea how and where she got it, but she had kept it for days and saved it just for him. He could not forget her shy face when the girl boldly kissed him for the first time upon their separation. In his pocket, he still kept the Chinese poem she gave to him:

> The time is so miserable
> That even flowers are shedding tears.
> Our parting is so sentimental
> Even the birds are crying with pain.

Thinking of his fiancée, K Hyoek's eyes filled with tears. Grief and loneliness overwhelmed him. He felt as if he were wandering on a vast plain and did not know what he should do to continue living. At night, he began singing in a low voice,

> I was born with poverty.
> The road ahead is full of tears and thorns.
> Tell me! Tell me! This bitter world!
> Biting the ground,
> I am crying but with no answer from this world.
> I can endure hunger by clenching my teeth.
> But how can I bear the insult and scorn
> That I receive every day?[2]
> Tell me! Tell me! This heartless world!
> How can I bear the insult and scorn
> That I receive every day?[2]

18. The Mongolia Route

I feel at home in Yanbian Korean Autonomous Prefecture. It resembles my hometown in Southern China, where boys herd cows by the creeks and girls carry a basket to collect weeds for the livestock. In Northeast China, people traditionally grow wheat, corn, millet and sorghum. But Yanbian people are diligent. They have created miracles by cultivating rice in the harsh weather conditions of Northeast China; people here eat good rice all year 'round. During China's Great Cultural Revolution, thousands upon thousands of Shanghai youths were forced here to undergo "reeducation." Many eventually fell in love with Yanbian and refused to return to Shanghai when they could at the end of the Revolution in 1976.

In Yanbian, signs on the roads, stores and government buildings are all in two languages. And newspapers, radio and TV stations use both Chinese and Korean. Many Korean restaurants serve Korean specialties such as chafing dishes and cold noodles.

Fashion stores fill the cities and busy shopping streets are everywhere.

Thousands upon thousands of North Koreans continue to risk their lives, crossing the Yalu and Tumen rivers to come to Yanbian Korean Autonomous Prefecture to seek hope and a better life.

"How many North Koreans have escaped to this side?" I ask Xiao Len the old question again.

"Many," comes his usual reply, "about five or six hide in every village."

The earliest escapees were mainly men. They worked very hard to store up grain and save money. When they had enough, they would sneak back to North Korea to feed their families. Like thousands of others, Kim Ron crossed the Tumen River to borrow food from his Chinese relatives.

143

The paper plant that he had worked in was shut down in 1995. When he came back to China for a second time, he was arrested and sent back. On his way to the labor camp, he ran away, and in January 2000 arrived in Tumen for the third time. When he reached the bank on the China side, he was so exhausted that he could not stand up. He made up his mind never to go back to North Korea again.

However, things have changed rapidly. In recent years, most of the escapees are women and children. Their fate is much more tragic.

It is hard to find an accurate answer to how many North Koreans are in China now because most of them live and work underground for private businesses. Through my visits to villages like Cold Water, numerous interviews with the locals and escapees, and collection of bits and pieces from local newspapers and magazines, I have concluded that at least 300,000 North Koreans are scattered throughout China's Northeast. Because of language barriers and cultural differences, most North Korean escapees still prefer the Korean communities of Yanbian, although some escape to the inland cities as far as Dailian and Beijing.

As more and more North Korean escapees "invade" the Prefecture, many local Chinese are growing tired of them. One time, Xiao Len surprises me by saying that Yanbian people don't like the North Koreans: "They are not worth our help."

Xiao Len is not a selfish man. He used to shed tears for those captured and forced back to face brutal punishment across the Tumen River. He also gave the North Koreans money and free rides to help them find living quarters and jobs.

"They are not grateful. And what is worse, they steal, rob, whore and sometimes kill our folks," he now says indifferently.

It has almost become a local custom for households to leave food and clothes outdoors for the escapees and for the North Korean border guards who cross the River to rob. During my stay in Yanbian, a group of North Korean men stopped a passenger vehicle and stripped the travelers of all their belongings. With some cash, they would immediately visit the "Three-Company" girls working in restaurants, salons, inns and public bathhouses. Many local Chinese youths scorn them, calling them "hungry wolves" and "trash people." Xiao Len has changed his mind, agreeing that the Chinese policemen should send them back.

However, not all the North Korean escapees are "hungry wolves."

A female North Korean doctor says, "I left North Korea not because I starved but because I did not like the dictatorial regime." Today, people have grown more and more indifferent to socialist values. As communist ethics have weakened, people of all rank run away from North Korea: military officers, journalists, doctors, and businessmen who possess special permits to do business in China. Many of the defectors are North Korea's elite, who have enough money to bribe the border guards to let them pass the Yalu and Tumen rivers. For them, strong political dissatisfaction and hatred of the existing regime is the driving force behind their defection. Fifteen percent of the escapees are members of the Korean Workers Party. Twenty percent believe that the North Korean government is responsible for the great famine. Seventy-seven percent say that North Korea cannot get through the famine by totally relying on itself, by sticking to the Juche theory of isolationist self-reliance.[1] Former Workers Party secretary Huang Jang-yop, who defected to the South in 1997, goes even further. He says that North Korea does not even have a socialist system, but rather a modern version of feudalism. A rigid vertical hierarchy remains the prime feature of society, with Kim Jong Il sitting at the top of the ladder.[2] Resentment of Kim Jong Il among the intellectuals has grown strong. They say that he should die, because if he does not, then everyone else will. They hate him but dare not speak out in North Korea.

"Look at North Korea!" Lee Min-bok, the former agricultural researcher says angrily "Along the southern border, no one can go through the mine-ridden and heavily guarded DMZ. High barbed wire and machine guns 'protect' North Korean coasts from the east to the west. To break the blockade and escape from the coast is riskier than crossing the Pacific Ocean by boat. This leaves the Korea-China border as the only route, but troops patrol the border day and night to stop the flood of flight…."

Since the beginning of 1999 Kim Jong Il has restored a small portion of rationed food to comfort the hungry population, while upgrading the punishment for those who still want to escape. In some of the provincial camps, the death rate is as high as one hundred percent. Kim Jong Il once told his son Kim Jon Nam that in order to sustain the family's rule of the country, the future successor must know how to stop the massive flight to China and other countries. Kim Jong Il knows that the border transgressors who first look for food will soon become political dissidents once they taste even just a little bit of the freedom and liberty across the border.

For many escapees, especially the educated, China's Yanbian Korean Autonomous Prefecture is only their first stop. Living at the bottom of society, exploited by all means but still in constant fear of arrest, they only want to make enough money so that they can go to South Korea. But they complain that in the earlier days, the South Korean government welcomed the Northerners because it would use their cases to boast its superior political system. In recent years, with millions of North Koreans wanting to go to the South, the South Korean government is reluctant to accept them. When the desperate North Korean escapees risk their lives and finally arrive at the South Korean Embassy in Beijing, the answer they get from their South Korean brothers and sisters is, "Go away as quickly as possible so you won't be caught by the Chinese policemen!"

Some are so hopeless at that point that they attempt to kill them-selves by swallowing poison that they carried with them in front of the South Korean officials. However, many, such as Lee Min-bok, are deter-mined to seek freedom at whatever cost. During his long years of exile, the former agricultural researcher was jailed in four countries before he eventually arrived in Seoul. He is angry with the South Korean officials: "I didn't trust those ... South Korean government officials so I applied directly to the UNHCR for refugee status in Russia. At last, I was approved as the first refugee from North Korea. The South Korean Embassy officials, upon hearing the news, scolded me angrily, 'Why did you damage our image by taking your case directly to the U.N.?'"

In 1994 and again in 1999, the South Korean government announced that it would allow any North Korean refugee to enter into the country from anywhere in the world. But the North Korean escapees suspect that the South is paying only lip service, because it has joined the Chinese gov-ernment in refusing to recognize the North Koreans as refugees. The aban-doned North Koreans, women and children included, end up wandering in the dark city streets or in the remote villages of foreign countries, search-ing for food and safety. They are often the targets of the slave trade, sex-ual abuse or exploitation as unpaid workers, enduring the world's harshest living and working conditions.

The North Korean defectors severely criticize former President Kim Da-jung's "Sunshine Policy," which they say stresses reconciliation with the North Korean government rather than protecting the human rights of the North Korean people, "The North is tough in its political stand, receiv-ing free donations from the South while the South is begging for recon-ciliation. The North is employing 'Terrorism Politics' and the South 'Mahatma Politics.' The North is oppressing its people but the South is afraid of addressing the issue."[3]

The "Little South" of Yanbian, a border region once so peaceful, so friendly with such racial harmony, has turned bloody and dangerous even for the local Chinese. Chinese policemen patrol the streets, stopping sus-picious cars and people, and searching for the North Korean escapees door-to-door and house-to- house.[4] As reported, whenever the Korean Chinese gathered at a big church in Yanji, the capital of Yanbian, North Korean orphans would attend the service to seek help and friendship. However, plainclothes North Korean agents would wait and rush into the church on Sunday to catch the children.[5] A secret war is being waged in Yanbian between the aggressive Christian missionaries from South Korea, Japan, and America, and the security services of China and North Korea. The underground religious groups are risking arrest by smuggling the escapees out of China.

When I visit the border towns and villages, every house, be it Korean-styled with a rising roof, or a Han structure with a flat top, seems just like any other. But many disguised Christian houses receive the North Korean orphans, hide young women, and help the men to find safe places. This underground railway system also actively transports the escapees to the China-Mongolia border. The escape is easy. All people need to do is to take a train to the border and simply go through the barbed wire. From there, they will travel to the Mongolian capital city of Ulaanbaatar.

This Mongolia journey is a lot shorter than the previous route, which passed through China, Burma, Thailand, and Vietnam. Along that route, escapees also had to watch out for 25 guard posts along the border waiting for them. The Mongolia route became popular because the whole trip is only 1,000 kilometers, as compared to 5,000 kilometers on the Vietnam route.[6] It is also much easier for the North Korean escapees to break through the Mongolian border, since both governments control the deserted area loosely.

Although all of the escapees want to go to South Korea, only very few can reach their ultimate destination. During their period of exile, their footprints cover much of China, Russia, and even Western Europe.

In South Korea, the first stop for escapees is Hanawon, the "get-together camp" located in a pine forest thirty miles south of Seoul. There, each escapee will get a resettlement compensation of $28,000 and receive instruction in English and computer skills.

But the new life awaiting these North Koreans is filled with alienation, challenge and discrimination. Having lived in an extremely closed communist country, the defectors will find it difficult to adjust to the highly competitive capitalist society.

Although the economy in the South is thirty times stronger than that in the North, the Southerners are still afraid that the poor Northerners will share their wealth. In April 2002, during my visit to Seoul, I met a young banker, a graduate of the prestigious University of Seoul, in front of the central government building downtown. The well-dressed young man stopped in a street park to smoke a cigarette. When I asked him what he thought about the new arrivals from the North, he replied in fluent English,

"The South doesn't recognize medical degrees from the North. So, even doctors and the other highly educated are doing construction work or housekeeping. There is no way out for them. It is very sad that they have to take the jobs that we do not want, and live at the bottom of society. Years of their education and training are useless here."

He paused to smoke. "Personally, I don't welcome them because it will cost us more to feed them. Too many people like them are coming.... To be frank, I don't want the North Korean regime to fall although I hate the dictatorial government. It is a very evil government."

Just in the first few months of 2002, there have been about fifty new arrivals in Seoul. It was a record high. Today, about 2,000 North Koreans have resettled in South Korea. Once they are free themselves, the first thing the escapees would do is to hire an agent to help them bring their families to the South. And the South Korean government will pay for these expenses also.

A young Korean Airline stewardess smiles politely in answer to the question of whether she welcomes the defectors: "I have no time to think about them and I don't even know where their camp is outside Seoul. First of all, I have to make enough money to get married. I am already 26, but still single because of my job, because I have to make money. Everything is so expensive nowadays. It is not cheap living in Seoul. Our government gives each of them a lot of money to settle down while many of us are still struggling. Those people are not going to adapt well to our society. They are used to getting everything provided for by the government. Suddenly, they have to depend totally on their own. Too much freedom scares them...."

When the initial exultation at gaining freedom and a new life wanes, the new arrivals face daily reality. Missing their homeland, especially the loved ones they have left behind, they sing,

> In these troubles of life,
> I am escaping death.
> Although the desire is urgent,
> What is the use of a new life without a home?
> I am wandering here and there,
> But only missing the blue sky and
> Bright moon of my homeland.

PART III

The Failure of the Communist Utopia

19. *Seeking a Change*

The first frost followed by sleet has already closed in upon Yanbian in September. The numerous Korean restaurants nevertheless bustle with local customers. For 50 yuan, or six dollars, one can get a chafing dish — actually a small banquet with many courses. In the center of a short-legged table, the kneeling waitress places a hot pot of boiling meat soup. She throws into the rich gravy sliced meat, sausages, green vegetables, Tofu, shrimp, mushrooms, and many other delicacies. The whole room seems to be an ocean of food. Xiao Len, who has accompanied me throughout my journey along the border, keeps explaining, "This is our hospitality. In any restaurant in Yanbian, the helping is more than generous."

This is my last night in the region. The next day, I will take the trains back to Shanghai. From there, I will soon fly to the United States, where my family are anxiously waiting for my return. However, many questions from my North Korea trip remain in my mind: Will the North Korean people suffer forever? What is the future of North Korea? What should the rest of the world do about the government?

At my parents' apartment in Shanghai, I find a pile of documents available only to ranking officials of the Chinese Communist Party. Before he retired, my father was the head of a university in Shanghai. He could and still can read the "internal" materials that the ordinary Chinese cannot. While the Chinese government never openly criticizes North Korea and newspapers only report positive stories about the country, these internal documents give Chinese officials a more accurate image of the troubled country.

"Paralysis" is the best word to describe the economy of today's North

Korea. Declining by an average of five percent yearly, its collapse cannot be far away.

In the early nineties, as the former Soviet bloc fell to pieces, supplies of petroleum, food, and fertilizers to North Korea were stopped completely. Meanwhile, economic reforms swept Mainland China. The revolution succeeded based on late leader Deng Xiaoping's famous "Cat Theory": be it a black or white cat, it is a good cat as long as it can catch a mouse.

In order for China to get rich quickly, the practical Deng refused to export rice and oil to North Korea unless it paid all its outstanding debts. Free socialist support is no longer possible.

North Korea's shortage of pesticides and fertilizer sharply reduced its own agricultural production. Although suffering from successive flood and drought, the government could not borrow money to purchase emergency grain because of its poor credit ratings. Also, the country could not use its overvalued currency, which is not exchangeable in international markets.

North Korean peasants cannot take a share of the harvest home from the public fields. Everything must be left as it is. The government is then responsible for processing the crops and redistributing the grain to the peasants, depending on the number of persons in the family. Usually men's rations are bigger than women's and adults' are bigger than children's. Beginning in 1995, the government reduced the farmers' average grain ration from 167 kilograms per man per year to 107 kilograms. The sharp cut dampened the farmers' enthusiasm to produce more food to support the cities and industrial areas. First and foremost, they must survive themselves. The food they received from the government was far from enough for the families to live on. They started harvesting before the season. They hid the grain in their roofs, where the extra weight caused many farmhouses to collapse. This was an undeclared war between the central government and the individual farmers. In 1996, about half of the corn yield, nearly 1.3 million metric tons, went missing before the harvest. The government sent emergency troops to protect the harvest. However, farmers bribed the corn guards, as the hungry soldiers were called, who ended up helping the farmers conceal the grains.[1]

Like the Chinese peasants under Mao, every North Korean farmer had been given a small piece of private plot for growing household vegetables. To get more from the tiny piece of land, the farmers devote almost all their time, energy, and skills to cultivating it. They even climb to the steep and infertile mountaintops to open up secret new fields. The small patches, known as firefields, can be seen on mountaintops across the country. As a result, the collective lands are seriously neglected. The yield of grain continues dropping. The government had had to dispatch soldiers to replace the missing peasants to plant, grow and harvest the crops.

From 1992 to 1994, public food distributions shifted from the four eastern provinces of Hamgyong Buk-do, Hamgyong Nam-do, Yangang, and Kangwon, which the government considers less important politically and militarily, to the western regions, where Pyongyang is located. Food supplies to the four provinces first became sporadic, and then stopped completely. In 1996, the county governments throughout the country were given the responsibility to feed their populations.

"If county administrators were particularly skillful and energetic, fewer people died; if bureaucratic and lethargic, the effect of the famine was acute," said Sue Lautze, an independent food observer, in June 1996.[2]

"The food crisis was so grave that even rations in Pyongyang dwindled to 300 grams (0.8 lbs) a day per person in 1996, and have ceased altogether in the provinces," confirms Hwang Jang-yop, former Korean Workers Party secretary.[3]

Early 1997 saw the peak of the famine. Kim Jong Il declared martial law on September 27 and created 927 detention camps in each county to jail people who traveled without permits.

In 1998, even the county food system collapsed, and it was up to each individual family to feed itself. Although Kim Jong Il believed that privatization would make people less dependent on the Workers Party and endanger the socialist system in North Korea, he finally accepted the idea, having no other option.

City workers and miners, who had relied on the public food distribution system for the past fifty years, were hit the hardest. With no salary or reduced wages, they could not afford the black market prices; a kilogram of corn would cost an average worker his monthly salary.

In 1999, China suffered from some of the most extensive flooding in its history, and the corn harvest was reduced by 70 to 90 percent. Meanwhile, North Korea had exhausted its sources of timber and scrap metal, which were used to trade for Chinese corn. As a result, grain prices in the black markets soared and caused a new round of deaths in the mountainous areas.

While famines traditionally have been economic phenomena with political and public health consequences, in totalitarian regimes where economics is subordinated to ideology, famines can be politically driven. Andrew Natsios, assistant administrator for the U.S. Agency for International Development's (USAID's) Bureau of Food and Humanitarian Assistance, says, "Despite manipulation and control, who lives and who dies is ultimately determined by microeconomic forces affecting specific regions, ages, incomes, and job groups differently, complicated by local food market prices."[4]

Guide Kim once compared the existing starvation in North Korea with the one Leningrad suffered during the Second World War, when the Germans surrounded the city for 900 days and countless Russians died from hunger. But Guide Kim said that the dear leader Kim Jong Il had led the country through the most difficult period.

What had Kim Jong Il done?

In 1994, immediately after the death of his father, Kim Jong Il started the "Bitter Long March," calling on the people to tighten their belts and prepare for the worst. He urged every North Korean citizen to take the national crisis as a battle to protect socialism. A popular song was written to inspire people,

> Coward! If you are afraid, just get away!
> We shall safeguard the red banner to the very end![5]

Meanwhile, Kim Jong Il made as many as 200 inspections of the People's Army to reassure the military, promising repeatedly that its food supply is always guaranteed, even if other people have nothing to eat at all. Kim Jong Il is Chairman of the National Defense Commission in addition to his other supreme title, General Secretary of the Korean Workers Party. Like Stalin and Mao Zedong, Kim Jong Il understands that as long as he controls the army, he will secure his absolute power and be able to rule the country with an iron hand.

With loyalty from the military as a strong foundation, Kim Jong Il is concentrating on a strategy to bring North Korea out of the economic nightmare. In the past, he had despised China's economic openness, calling the agricultural revolution "the death of socialism," and "betrayal of Communism." He regarded the Chinese Communist Party as revisionists of Marxism-Leninism and showed no interest in following China. In fact, Kim Jong Il did not even allow the topic of economic reforms to be discussed. Visitors returning from China could only report its problems, such as the huge army of unemployed workers produced by the privatization of state-run enterprises, the trafficking in women and children, and the prevalence of prostitution. Afraid of being labeled as "reactionaries," Kim's top party secretaries, such as Kim Yongsoon and Han Sungryong, kept their mouths shut even if they deeply believed that economic reform was not only necessary but also urgent for North Korea.[6]

Since the start of his Bitter Long March, Kim Jong Il has made some policy adjustments. First of all, he called for less intrusion of the Workers

Party into the economy. The Party would take care of ideology, but government agencies would be more responsible for the daily business. This means that he is loosening the Party's stiff ideological control, separating the Party and the government agencies, which are given more flexibility in making decisions regarding economic development. To provide some incentives to the farmers, Kim has increased the private plot to 0.02 hectares per family, allowing the peasants to sell their agricultural surplus harvested from the small plot at the black market. Every household can now raise five chickens and 25 rabbits.[7] Kim also sent city residents to help in the countryside with planting, harvesting, irrigation, and manure collecting. With more freedom to choose what kind of crops they can grow, to apply for loans from the banks, and to engage in small-scale trade with the Chinese, North Korean farmers harvested about four million tons of grain in the year 2000. The country gradually got over the worst of the famine. In October of the same year, Kim Jong Il declared the end of the Bitter Long March.

Guide Kim said proudly, "Our initial victory is a heavy blow to the popular theory in the West that North Korea will soon perish. This again proves the correctness of our dear leader Kim Jong Il's policies. North Korea will never disappear from the surface of the earth."

However, North Korea's economy is still highly planned and all economic activities still depend heavily upon the orders of the top leaders. The agricultural outlook remains weak, and the difficult economic situation has not changed much. North Korea has to undergo a fundamental revolution to provide the peasants with enough profit incentives.

Under the enormous pressure, Kim Jong Il has admitted the urgency of economic reform in North Korea. At the beginning of the new century, Kim hinted as much to the world, "We have entered a new epoch. We cannot live the old life anymore. We must change." But at the same time he also said, "Do not expect me to deviate from our principles,"[8] meaning that North Korea would continue to stick to Korean-style socialism.

The state-run *Worker's Daily* echoes Kim Jong Il: "We will continue to fight against revisionist ideology [referring to China's model] in all our departments, but we have recognized the new requirements set by the new century. In this new economic era, we will follow our principles to speed up our socialist construction."

However, not all his party officials support him. Kim Jong Il often complains, "I am tired of obsolete ideas and disgusted to see the old bureaucrats around me. These people like to follow established rules and are afraid of changes."[9]

He has replaced his old aides with young economic advisers and the aged and fearful senior vice premiers with energetic junior ones. However, Kim has not changed the most important criterion in selecting new officials: they must bear unconditional loyalty to him.

The Chinese government delegations to Pyongyang were quick to notice the changes. In the past, senior North Korean officials spoke endlessly about "confrontation," "getting prepared for the war." But in recent encounters, the new officials no longer criticize the "Japanese and American imperialists." Instead, they are eager to find a solution.

Today, the North Korean government has reached a dead end. Other than engaging in economic reform, it has no way out. And the reform must be carried out sooner rather than later.

Although North Korea has not yet adopted China's economic model, China's shocking economic achievements have deeply impressed Kim Jong Il. In May 2000, he secretly visited Beijing and upon his return appeared on television, praising China's new outlook.

In 2001, Kim stopped at the new Shanghai stock market in Pudong and toured a joint-venture car-assembly plant built by General Motors, as well as an NEC semiconductor factory. Modern technology shocked and amazed him. Back in North Korea, he described the changes in Shanghai as "earthshaking" and "breathtaking."[10] His last visit to the city had been in 1983, when Shanghai was still recovering from the disastrous Cultural Revolution. City residents lived in low hovels and carried coupons everywhere they went for rationed food and clothing. Today, however, Shanghai's splendid skyscrapers and new network of highways color the landscape and food piles up in the markets. Kim wanted Pyongyang to be just like Shanghai. If Shanghai can, why not Pyongyang?

Kim Jong Il showed his determination to follow China in September of 2001 when he held an extravagant welcome ceremony for visiting Chinese President Jiang Zemin. Girls and boys holding fresh flowers flooded Pyongyang's streets. People in holiday attire sang and danced on Kim Il Sung Square. People's Army soldiers goose-stepped in unison to show respect for their distinguished Chinese guest. Deafening cheers of welcome filled the air.

Even President Jiang did not expect this kind of reception, the biggest and most luxurious in the country's history. It even surpassed the lavish celebration of Kim Jong Il's own birthday.

The reform-minded Kim Jong Il has already promised the North Koreans that in five years he will provide computers and cell phones free for them. As a great fan of the Internet, he has applauded the invention: "Although the capitalists invented the Internet, the Internet itself does not belong to any class. Rather, the new tool provides an important opportunity to our people."[11]

Kim Jong Il (left) holds an extravagant welcome ceremony for visiting Chinese president Jiang Zemin in September 2001. In doing so, Kim shows his determination to follow China's footsteps and open up his country to the world during his lifetime (Xinhua News Agency).

Kim Jong Il realizes that only South Korea, with common ties of language and culture, can provide the technology and capital that North Korea needs most at present.

In recent years, he has started working to improve his relationship with the South. On June 13, 2000, Kim Jong Il and then South Korean president Kim Dae-jung met in Pyongyang. Holding Kim Dae-jung's hand, Kim Jong Il said, "This meeting is a very good beginning. Following this example, we can solve many other problems between our two countries. Let this day be remembered forever."

Kim Dae-jung replied, "Together, let us create history."

The summit earned Kim Dae-jung the Nobel Peace Prize, and Kim Jong Il was selected Man of the Year in *Time* magazine's Asian edition. Before him, only two Communist leaders— Deng Xiaoping and Mikhail Gorbechev— had won this honor.

From the end of the Korean War in 1953, for forty-eight years no mail, telephone or other direct means of communication had been allowed

On June 13, 2000, Kim Jong Il (right) and South Korean president Kim Dae-jung meet in Pyongyang, reopening dialogue after nearly half a century (Xinhua News Agency).

between private citizens of the two Koreas. But the declaration signed by both leaders on June 15, 2001, changed the situation. The two Koreas have allowed an initial group of 100 separated spouses from each side to visit Seoul and Pyongyang respectively. Separated family members from South Korea will eventually be allowed to visit their hometowns in the North. It is one of a series of goodwill gestures made by the two countries, and a major step towards reconciliation of a peninsula divided since 1945.

In Seoul, people welcomed the good news. Stores sold portraits of Kim Jong Il. A man who looks exactly like Kim became a star. He told reporters, "I don't know about politics, but for the ordinary people here in Seoul, we have good feelings towards Chairman Kim. When I walk on the streets, children ask me for autographs, and the adults smile at me, calling me 'Chairman of the National Defense Commission'..... Anyway, this is a good beginning for us to be friendly...."

However, after September 11, 2001, the North Korean government cancelled the scheduled reunion for October of the same year, blaming South Korea for issuing a nationwide security alert. As one South Korean says, "Every time we think we are going forward, we always seem to take a step back."

The reconciliation process, full of hope, came to a sudden halt.

20. Engaging the West

Kim Jong Il should not be underestimated, South Korean President Kim Dae-jung warns the world. Kim Jong Il has made it known that he would not hesitate to use nuclear, biological and chemical weapons against South Korea.[1] North Korea owns about 1,700 Scud missiles and has been exporting them to Iran, Syria, Pakistan, and Iraq for oil. North Korea provided 40 percent of Iran's weapons during the Iran-Iraq war. It also sold its own Scud rockets and transshipped Chinese Silkworm missiles to the Middle East. Recently, North Korea has developed and is deploying a long-range missile named Rodong-I, which can reach South Korea and Japan.[2]

Unlike previous U.S. administrations, which had relied on economic sanctions and political isolation, the Clinton administration's response to the North Korean threat was to engage the nation. From an American perspective, a stable, friendly Korean Peninsula would check China's growing influence in the region and strengthen the American military presence in East Asia. Kim Jong Il, for his part, wanted to establish ties with the United States so as to "set the U.S. against China, meanwhile forcing the Japanese to go along with all subsequent agreements and souring U.S.-South Korean relations at the same time," according to Kim's former party secretary, Hwang Jang-yop.[3]

In 1994, North Korea held talks in Geneva with the United States. On the issue of nuclear weapons, the two sides reached a deal: South Korea, Japan, the European Union and the United States would finance North Korea in building two nuclear power plants for civilian purposes and provide it annually with 500 metric tons of heavy fuel oil, worth $5 billion if it suspended its nuclear program, allowed periodic inspections and maintained a friendly relationship with the Western world. This deal would give North Korea enough energy to restore the economy and feed its people. But North Korea has not allowed any American inspectors to enter the country. It accuses the United States of not complying completely with these conditions.

Although some in the U.S. complained that the missile control accord is an empty contract that North Korea has no intention of observing, the Clinton administration continued its engagement policy. In October 2000, Cho Min-ro, First Vice Chairman of the National Defense Commission of North Korea, visited the United States as a special envoy for Kim Jong Il. While visiting Lucent Technologies, Cho told the Americans that North Korea is extremely interested in new technology. At the home of George Washington, Cho pointed out North Korea on a map of the world on the wall. During this visit, the United States and North Korea declared that they would end hostility towards each other and combine efforts to deal with international terrorism.

Following Cho's visit, Secretary of State Madeleine Albright traveled to North Korea to discuss a wide variety of issues, from weapons expansion and economic openness, to problems hindering the normalization of bilateral relations. Since Kim Jong Il is an avid fan of the NBA, Albright brought him a basketball autographed by Michael Jordan. After her arrival, Kim visited Albright personally at her hotel, an unprecedented move. When Albright told Kim that she was ready to receive his phone calls, he replied, "Why don't you give me your email address?"

During their meeting, Kim Jong Il promised Albright that North Korea would stop developing longer-range missiles. The United States agreed to withdraw part of its economic sanctions and provide the impoverished nation with further economic assistance. Kim also requested that more Korean Americans be sent to North Korea to teach English. In the past, those people were regarded as traitors and subject to execution if they came back.

Negotiations on new and verifiable agreements between the United States and North Korea continued, to "get rid of their missile technology. Over the time we would have moved on the whole range of weapons— gas, chemical, germs," as Albright says.

Other Western countries quickly followed the lead of the United States. In the past two years, altogether 13 out of the 15 members of the European Union, Canada, and Australia established diplomatic relations with North Korea. Scattered travelers from Western Europe could be spotted, although under strict supervision, in Pyongyang and Panmunjom.

In the eyes of Western business people, North Korea is like an

2000 年 10 月 25 日，金正日再次会见奥尔布赖特

Kim Jong Il and Madeleine Albright met on October 25, 2000, to discuss important issues that could lead to normalization of relations between the two countries (Xinhua News Agency).

untapped golden basin. The Association of International Businesses, based in Beijing, declared breathlessly, "Power, mining and minerals are all areas where the DPRK (North Korea) has resources, and therefore, there is the potential to get money or collateral out in exchange for foreign income."[4]

France showed interest in building the country's communications system. It has already discussed with the government its plans for replacing North Korea's old equipment. Germany promised to provide beef, and its corporations eyed the machinery, energy, and finance sectors with great interest. Holland had signed a contract with North Korea early in 1998 to set up a power plant. The ABB group of Sweden agreed to modernize the nation's obsolete electricity wires.

But U.S. policy changed abruptly after George W. Bush took office in 2001. He spoke about Kim Jong Il with contempt: "A leader who leaves his own country in starvation can't get trust from others."

In retaliation, Kim Jong Il said that he would continue to develop strategic satellites. But North Korea would not threaten those countries that respect its sovereignty. In other words, he says he is not afraid of confrontation with hostile countries like the U.S.

President Bush insists that in order for the United States to continue talks, North Korea must stop making and exporting missiles, reduce the military force stationed along the DMZ, and allow the United States to inspect its nuclear facilities.

However, deliveries of fuel oil to generate electricity in North Korea "were constantly late and construction of the two nuclear reactors fell five years behind schedule. The 1994 framework was to be followed by other steps which the United States has never taken. We hoped their regime would collapse before we ever had to deliver on the deal," says Joseph Cirincione, director of the nuclear nonproliferation program at the Carnegie Endowment for International Peace in Washington.[5] But the North Korean government has proven surprisingly durable.

Leon Sigal, director of the Northeast Asia Cooperative Security Project at the Social Science Research Council in New York, also says, "We did not live up to our obligations in return," after getting "upfront" what the U.S. wanted in 1994.[6]

In November 2002, the North Korean government, after years of denying it, admits to having revived its nuclear building program.[7]

A recent survey shows that a majority of Americans feel that only through continued negotiations can the nuclear threat from North Korea be diminished.[8]

Which road will America follow?

21. *Beautifying Terrorism*

In his State of the Union address on January 24, 2001, President Bush named North Korea as part of an "axis of evil" and the world's number-one merchant of ballistic missiles. President Bush has a reason to target North Korea in his global war against terrorism.

Despite his intention to develop relations with the West, Kim Jong Il has always believed that North Korea's best interests could be attained only through force.

Since 1953, North Korean agents have abducted 3,790 South Koreans and engaged in about 420,000 terrorist incidents against the South. They were responsible for a raid on the presidential residence in Seoul in January 1968, leading to the death of seven. They broke into the Ulchin-Samchok area of South Korea in October 1968, killing 20 commandos. In 1983, they planted a bomb in Burma (Myanmar) that killed four visiting South Korean cabinet ministers. They plotted the midair explosion of a Korean Air passenger jet over the Bay of Bengal in November 1987 which took the lives of all 115 people aboard.

In 1994, a South Korean missionary working in China disappeared. Later, he showed up on North Korean television portrayed as a defector. Three Korean-Chinese children living in Beijing were abducted in 1995 because their father, a former prisoner in North Korea, had criticized its human-rights violations in the Japanese media.

In November 1997, several North Korean spies arrested by the South confessed that they had kidnapped three South Korean high school students in 1978 and trained them to work for the North.

On February 5, 1997, Yi Han-yeong, nephew of Kim Jong Il's ex-wife, who had defected to the South and was living in Seoul, was found dead in front of the elevator at his apartment building. His assassins, a pair named Cho Jeong-nam and Gang Yeong-jeong, from North Korea's Society and Culture Department, received heroic titles upon their return. In Pyongyang, they reportedly underwent plastic surgery to prepare them for future assassinations in the South.

In September 1996, a North Korean submarine tried to land armed agents into the South. When it hit a reef and floated to the surface, several commandoes committed suicide. Others refused to surrender. They fought to the last drop of blood, killing several South Korean soldiers.

The country has also conducted terrorist activities in Japan. The Japanese media estimates that as many as twenty of its citizens may have been kidnapped to North Korea.

On November 15, 1977, a sweet-faced girl named Megumi disappeared on her way back from badminton practice. More than two decades later, news confirmed that the North Korean agents abducted her, together with eleven others, to teach Japanese back in North Korea. Among the abducted were also a club hostess, a dating couple who went to the seaside to watch a sunset, a cook who was lured to a North Korean ship, and Keiko Arimoto, a college student who was job-hunting in Denmark in 1983.[1]

Today, eight out of the twelve abducted, including Megumi, are dead. In November 2002, Kim Jong Il gave the news personally to visiting Japanese Prime minister Junichiro Koizumi.

Shibata Kozo and his wife Shin Sung Suk, both Japanese citizens, resettled in North Korea in 1960. The government arrested Shibata two years later after he staged a demonstration against discrimination and poor treatment. He was imprisoned for nearly thirty years. In 1995, North Korean officials declared that Shibata Kozo, his wife and children had all died in a train accident.

Japanese citizens Cho Ho Pyong and his wife Koike Hideko and their three young children were killed in 1972 while trying to leave North Korea. The government accused Cho of attempting to escape from a detention center, where he had been held for spying.

North Korean agents have also increased their operations in China, trying to capture escapees and their benefactors.[2] Cho Wonchol, a Korean Chinese who used to send goods back to his relatives in North Korea, was abducted in Tumen. His whereabouts are still unknown.

When Hwang Jang-yop, the number-three party official in the North Korean government, sought asylum at the South Korean Embassy in Beijing in 1997, agents dispatched from North Korea's Beijing embassy stormed the building, attempting to capture Hwang dead or alive. This prompted

The South Korean Embassy in Beijing is heavily guarded, to prevent North Korean agents from intruding. It is also impossible for North Korean defectors to raid it. The historic event in Prague where more than 1,100 East German defectors climbed over the fence of the West German Embassy, leading to the collapse of the Berlin Wall, is unlikely to happen in Beijing (Xinhua News Agency).

the Chinese government to set up barricades and to station police around the South Korean Embassy. Now, Hwang stays in South Korea, still living under heavy security.

In recent years, many resettled North Korean defectors living in South Korea have been reported missing.[3] One man surnamed Kim, a former senior official with the Korean Workers Party, left on a trip to China six months ago and never came back.

North Korea also supports terrorist organizations around the world, or "supporting the world revolution," as it calls it. Following Mao's example in the sixties, today's North Korea wants to be the headquarters of the world revolution. From 1969 to 1971, militants in Burundi and Rwanda tried to assassinate their national leaders. North Korea had armed and trained them. In 1982, Israel arrested some 80 terrorists in Lebanon. Among them were 24 North Koreans. In July 1997, 175 North Korean military instructors were advising guerrilla groups in Tanzania and Uganda.[4]

The Society and Culture Department, the United Front Department, the External Intelligence Investigation Department, and the Operations Department, together with the Reconnaissance Bureau of the Korean Armed Forces Ministry, work to plan and carry out the terrorist operations. Kim Jong Il has personally directed these government branches since 1974.

In 2001, the United States again put North Korea on its list of "rogue" nations, along with Iraq, Iran, Syria, and Libya. With such a title placed upon it, North Korea could not receive economic aid and cheap bank loans from the World Bank and other international financial organizations. Its government cried foul, demanding that the U.S. take the country off the list.

"As soon as they remove it, even tomorrow," a North Korean official says, "we would establish ties with the U.S."[5]

But the United States believes diplomatic relations can be restored only after four conditions have been met.

1. North Korea must sign a written pledge that it will never again engage in terrorist activities.
2. It must provide evidence showing that it has not engaged in any such activities in the past six months.
3. It must join an international pact created to prevent such activities.
4. It must take action to deal with its past terrorist activities.

Specifically, the U.S. has asked Pyongyang to surrender the Japanese Red Army, which still hides in North Korea after hijacking a Japan Airlines carrier in 1970. The North Koreans have flatly declined to do so.

Speaking at an international conference on biological weapons held in Geneva, John R. Bolton, the United States Undersecretary of State for Arms Control, said that North Korea has made a "dedicated national-level effort" to acquire germ weapons. Known as "the poor man's atom bomb," germ weapons are powerful and destructive. Experts say that if, for instance, a smallpox weapon were to be used, half of the world population under the age of twenty, who have not been vaccinated, could be killed.

"North Korea could likely produce sufficient quantities of biological agents for military purposes within weeks of a decision to do so," Bolton warns.

Where does this leave the civilized world?

22. Starve the Regime to Death?

What should the rest of the world do about North Korea? Should we stop all the international food aid and starve the regime to death, as one theory has insisted for years? Or should we engage it and help the country transform on its own?

Looking back, the world has provided more than generous support ever since the North Korean government appealed for international help in 1995.

Following a flood in 2001 that drowned crops and homes and destroyed roads and bridges, the World Food Program (WFP) rushed emergency food aid to tens of thousands of people in Kangwon Prefecture in the southeast. It was the single largest such operation worldwide, bigger even than the urgent monthly relief to Afghanistan.[1]

From 1995 to 1996, food aid to North Korea amounted to 903,374 tons. That figure increased to 11,171,665 tons from 1996 to 1997, and then went up to 11,321,528 tons from 1997 to 1998.

Who donated the food?

The assistance came primarily from the United States, the European Union, China, Japan, and South Korea.

In Yanbian Korean Autonomous Prefecture, a Korean-Chinese lady who has just come back from visiting her relatives in North Korea tells me that with the generous international aid, some of the hardest-hit miners and their families can receive food rations again, even though they last only twenty days a month. Children are beginning to go to school again, and smiles have replaced the sad look on adults' colorless faces.

Supporters of engagement believe that the international food support program is a "poisonous carrot," because it helps shake people's confidence in the government. Most North Koreans knew nothing about foreign assistance before. They knew only that U.S. troops gathered at the China border, preparing to invade the country, and South Korea, meanwhile, was sending them rice tainted with cyanide poison. Living a life hardly imaginable by people in other countries, ordinary North Koreans believed that North Korea is safe, and the rest of the world dangerous and miserable.

Kim Jong Il obviously does not like the food assistance program. He said on June 19, 1997, "The imperialists give us one thing while taking a hundred things away from us."[2] He feels that the food program threatens the Party's propaganda about the outside capitalist world.

With the return of rations, Kim Jong Il has also tightened the Party's ideological control and started conducting routine ideological checks. He orders that every week people must attend an "Ideological Review." He wants to know everything, including things that people do in the bathroom.

Here is a political joke about how people in North Korea are forced to criticize themselves and denounce others.

> Last night, comrade Lee stole a sack of valuable coal.
>
> Lee's colleagues criticize him: "It is a serious crime because he shows no respect to our Dear Leader. What he has done is anti-party, anti-revolution and anti-socialism. We agree that Comrade Lee can't heat his home without coal, but we cannot tolerate his selfishness. He forgets that our socialist economy is suffering from temporary difficulties and shows no intention to protect it. We must not be sympathetic to his behavior."
>
> Ten days' worth of grain is taken away from Comrade Lee's already meager rations. To survive, the miner may just have to steal again.

Today, when some argue about whether the international food program has propped up the North Korean government or weakened it, others argue that, morally and ethically, the world should distinguish the millions of innocent North Korean people from their dictatorial leaders.

"This hardworking moral people deserves better than it has gotten from a United States that has been deeply involved in the lives of both Koreas for half a century but knows them not,"[3] one American scholar says.

After all, can the North Korean government be starved to death if the world stops the generous international food support?

Looking back at the history of other communist states like the Soviet Union and China, similar mass starvations did not cause their governments to fall even with the deaths of millions. On the contrary, famine strengthened the rulers' iron-fisted control.

In 1931, Stalin pushed for his agricultural collectivization in the Soviet Union, but met with strong resistance from well-off Ukrainian peasants. To enforce his policies, Stalin sent out 100,000 Moscow agents, who "locked up [the] food and guarded it from the people. The grain collectors took not only the wheat from the peasants but stripped them of all food. In one village near Odessa, they collected all the grain, potatoes, and beets to the last kilogram and in other places they even took half-baked loaves of bread from the stove."[4] This resulted in a great man-made famine, which lasted from 1931 to 1933, turning the breadbasket of Ukraine into a living hell.

Arthur Koestler, a famous writer about the Soviets, wrote of "...hordes of families in rags begging at the railway stations, the women lifting up to the compartment window their starving brats, which, with drumstick limbs, big cadaverous heads and puffed bellies, looked like embryos out of alcohol bottles...."[5]

Desperate people ate mice, rats, sparrows, ants, earthworms, leather shoes, shoe soles, glue, old felt and furs. An American traveler, Carveth Wells, saw children eating grass. Adults killed and ate their own offspring. Stalin's punishment was harsh: anyone who stole would be killed at once. Farmers died in huge numbers and those who still breathed fled to the train station, boarding any train, hoping to survive the coming winter. Every morning, about 250 corpses and those still dying were removed from the station and thrown into pits in the outskirts, where bodies heaped.

The secret was exposed only after Stalin died: at the peak of the famine, about 25,000 people died daily and total deaths were estimated to be from five to eight million. As one Russian woman in Poltava said, "No war ever took from us so many people." The death toll in the 1932–33 famine was higher than that of any country which fought in the First World War.[6] The death rate, 32,680,700 in January 1932, was about 25 percent of Ukraine's population.

But mankind did not learn. My father, a political science scholar, still remembers China's great famine clearly. In 1959, when he worked at Harbin Industrial University, the Soviet tragedy repeated itself in China. Mao Zedong's Great Leap Forward program and the People's Commune system caused an acute shortage of food. Mao had believed false reports from local officials that the grain yield for each hectare was over 100,000 kilograms, 600 times higher than the real figure.[7] When peasants could not hand in so much food, Mao started the Struggle Against Harvest Cheating. The People's Commune officials took away from the peasants all their storage of food, seeds, even forage for livestock. In Xinyang County, Henan Province in a former model commune set up personally by Mao during the Great Leap Forward program for the whole country to learn from, all the public canteens, where the peasants ate together for free, had to shut down, with nothing to serve. In one village, there was not a single grain in sight for eighty days. Everything edible had been eaten, including weeds from thatched roofs, cotton from coats, pants, vine leaves, fine dirt, and even young humans. But Mao refused to aid the starving peasants, whom he deemed low and worthless. He once said that even if half of the country's 600 million people perished, China would still have 300 million, still the biggest population in the world.

Although the Chinese government claimed, and still claims, that the three-year famine was caused by natural disasters, my father said that the weather was favorable from 1959 to 1961. The famine was totally man-made. As millions of Chinese peasants lay dying, Mao continued to export grains in exchange for foreign currency to build up his nuclear bombs, which were successfully exploded shortly after the great famine. Hunger wiped out village after village. About 40 million Chinese died in the three-year catastrophe. Most were peasants whose crops were taken away to support the cities.

"Famine no matter how great doesn't bring about the collapse of [these governments]. Mao's regime didn't disintegrate; instead the famine may have helped strengthen its hold over the country. Nor did Stalin fall from power after his famine, and he went on to institute the Great Terror, purging millions suspected of disloyalty."[8]

Today, Kim Jong Il's brutality at least equals that of Stalin and Mao, if not surpassing theirs. Ordinary people throughout North Korea are desperately waiting for food coming from the countryside, but not much comes. Workers and miners simply starve silently at home, hoping for the best but waiting for death. From big cities to rural towns, from Pyongyang's apartment buildings to Manpo's peasant cottages, all stand lifeless. Death lurks everywhere.

A satellite photo capturing the Korean peninsula at night tells it all. North China and South Korea are a blaze of lights. However, North Korea is totally in the dark. Even the fishing fleets in the Sea of Japan give off far more illumination. In that deadly darkness, 23 million people, including malnourished children, are struggling silently. How can a hospital emergency room save lives without electricity?

But Kim Jong Il would not mind even if 70 percent of the country's population died, just as Mao was ready to let half his people perish.

Today, no one knows exactly how many North Koreans have already died since the famine started in early nineties, because the government hides all information. After all, the famine is a secret one. Estimates vary.

Extensive interviews of the Korean escapees in China's Yanbian Korean Autonomous Prefecture by the Korean Buddhist Sharing Movement confirm that North Korea's great famine occurred first in the urban and mining areas in the northern region. In some mountainous areas, the death rates are as high as 26 to 28 percent.[9]

Former party secretary Hwang Jang-yop claims, "In November 1996, I was very concerned about the economy and asked a top official how many people had starved to death. He replied, 'In 1995, about 500,000 people starved to death including 50,000 party cadres. In 1996, about one million people are estimated to have starved to death. In 1997, about two million people would starve to death if no international aid were provided.'"[10]

Hwang himself estimated later in interviews with the South Korean media that about 2.5 million people had succumbed since 1995, with one million deaths in 1997 alone.

In 1998, the United Nations concluded that about 3.5 million people out of an entire population of 23 million have perished. The mortality rate, at 15 percent, is much higher than that of the Soviet and China famines, which were at approximately 5 percent and 6 percent, respectively.

Unfortunately, the death rate for the North Koreans is still growing.

Since October 2002, after the North Korean government openly admitted that it had continued its nuclear weapons program, many international food donors refused to give more. Kathi Zellweger, the director of the International Co-operation for Caritas-Hong Kong, made an appeal: "From November 1, the money from donors ran out and Caritas must stop giving nutritional biscuits to three million children. If we get no more pledges by January, 1.5 million pregnant mothers and their children will also be affected."

She pointed out that one-third of the North Korean population relies on food aid. As the head of the world's biggest non-government contributor of aid to North Korea, Kathi reminds people that "a hungry child knows nothing of politics. The average seven-year-old boy in South Korea is 125 cm tall and weighs 26 kg, while his cousin in the north is 105 cm tall and weighs 16 kg. There is chronic malnutrition everywhere that impairs both physical and mental growth.... There is surplus food everywhere — in Japan, China and Russia, not to speak of Europe and the United States. Think how much we waste. I saw old women with clothes bags picking up individual grains of rice out of the field after the harvest. They know that hard times are ahead."

James Morris, the U.N. World Food Program's executive director, also warns that North Korea's food crisis has reached a critical level. Without continuous international food aid, four million out of the 5.5 million hungry children will die of starvation by the end of next year.

"This famine, which resembles so closely the famine in China, may be even more deadly. It is not over yet, and before it is, the death toll in North Korea may represent a larger proportion of the population than the Chinese famine. Never before has a regime been willing to allow its own people to perish in such numbers around the monuments to a failed utopia,"[11] British journalist Jasper Becker angrily accuses.

Today, the North Korean government is holding its entire people hostage. Human lives have never been so valueless.

23. Rise in Arms?

"When 40 million Chinese died from the man-made famine, did people think about overthrowing Mao's dictatorship?" I ask my father.

"For people who have never lived under communist rule, it is hard to imagine why people would rather bear the sufferings than stand up in arms. As long as the rulers control the army, people must be obedient as lambs. China has an old saying, 'If the emperor wants me to die, I have no choice but to die.' Imagine if Mao believed that I was not loyal to him and should die, could I survive his order? Absolutely not! I guess the same applies to the North Koreans. Turbulence from below is impossible. Change must start at the top."

Although many North Koreans do in fact hate the government, they can do nothing. Under strict one-party rule and tight military control, terror envelops the country. Propaganda has bombarded every aspect of people's lives. Police arrest anyone who complains. Soldiers patrol the streets. Any attempt to overthrow the regime would be quickly repressed. Dr. Vollertsen, who has worked in North Korea for more than a year, concludes, "the people can't help themselves. They are brainwashed, and too afraid to be able to overthrow their rulers."

North Korean escapees have also expressed their fears; "To revolt? It's unthinkable! If you raise your head, it is chopped. You and your family."

Kim Jong Il's government secretly killed Jun, a young Pyongyang college student, for starting an anti-government organization. For years, Jun's family had lived on nothing but grass roots and tree-bark soup. When Jun's wife became pregnant, he quit school to collect firewood in the deep mountains, and then sold it in the black market for some food. In 1995, starvation stopped everything from functioning. As in all famines, disease always goes hand-in-hand with starvation. Jun's parents died and his pregnant wife was bedridden. Jun sold everything in the house to save his wife. The young couple encouraged each other that once the winter was over, swallows would come back and new grass would spring up from the ground. They could eat the new plants and go on living. In a month, a baby would be born and they would smile to see the fruit of their love. Jun told his wife that he would sing a cradlesong for the baby. His wife held his hands and smiled.

The next day, on his way back home from the mountain, he saw a dead crow. Overjoyed, he picked up the bird and rushed home. He would cook the bird in a soup for his wife. But when he got home, his wife was unconscious. On the way to the hospital, she stopped breathing.

Grief-stricken, Jun fell to the ground and asked himself millions of questions. He wanted to know why his parents and young wife had to starve to death. He wanted to know why North Korean people had to live in such difficulty. He began traveling all over the country. Wherever he went, he saw unfortunate people just like him. He realized that the Juche ideology was nothing but a scam. He talked to people, held secret meetings and formed an underground organization against the Workers Party. But in 1997, the Hyaeryeong Security Bureau arrested him. When he was taken out for execution, he left the world with these words: "We must act and build our own paradise! No one will do it for us, only we ourselves! No one will liberate us but we ourselves!"

In May and June of 2000, Kim Jong Il executed more than thirty senior party officials and merchants in the border city of Hyesan. Twelve of them were shot in public. Im Sang-gil, an eyewitness now living in South Korea, says, "The residents were somewhat puzzled because most of those to be executed were men of power or wealth.... More than 10,000 people gathered to watch the executions."

The "criminals" faced charges of embezzlement, illicit accumulation of wealth, and smuggling. They were also accused of engaging in espionage activities to help people flee to China or arranging reunions in China for separated North and South Korean families.

Previously, such "criminals" were fastened to poles and shot from a certain distance. But in the Hyesan execution, they were made to kneel down and were shot in the head at point-blank range. The crowd, including many children, was frightened to the point of crying. Purges followed. About 100 senior officials were imprisoned and sent to labor camps, and their families were exiled.

Cho Young Chol, a former military instructor who fled to the South in 1998, tells horrible stories about prison torment and group executions. He and his elder brother were taken to the State Security Agency Prison. His brother was beaten so badly that his arm and limb joints were dislocated and all his teeth were broken. His face was disfigured beyond recognition. Cho was put down on a table naked and hit with electric shocks. He saw one inmate killed instantly when struck on the head with an iron hook. Many died during the brutal tortures. In less than two weeks, Cho's weight was reduced from 67 kg to 46 kg. His entire body was swollen.

"On July 1, 1998," he recalls, "six people, among them my elder brother, were executed in public under Namsan Bridge. In the past, public executions were generally limited to economic criminals. Political offenders were killed in secret. And it was quite rare to see the State Security Agency itself performing the public executions. But in this public execution, they shot my elder brother so many times that his upper body was all but unrecognizable. Before he was taken out of the prison, I saw that his mouth and lips were all covered with wounds. With his teeth all broken, his spine injured and arms and limbs dangling, he was carried out by two security guards. 'At least, you must stay alive and look after our parents,' were the last words he had for me."[1]

Despite these high-handed tactics to eliminate any resistance, there were still attempts to overthrow Kim Jong Il.

Hamhung, the country's largest industrial city, was hit hardest by the food shortage. About 500,000 factory workers had died from hunger in 1995. There, the Sixth Corps of the People's Army launched a failed coup against Kim Jong Il. Following the plot, Kim executed many of the officers, and replaced old soldiers with new ones who swore absolute loyalty to him. Kim imposed martial law at the peak of the famine in 1996 and 1997.[2] Rumors said he avoided attending military drills where live ammunition was used and slept at a different place every night. "A wily hare has three burrows—a crafty person has more than one hideout."

In September 1997, Kim put his agriculture minister, Suh Kwan Hei, and seven others to death before a massive crowd. He accused them of being "spies of the American imperialists." The execution was actually the defeat of an assassination attempt. After Suh's execution, Kim ordered the remains of Kim Man Kum, the former premier who had recommended Suh as his successor, removed from the Patriots Cemetery. Soldiers fired at the bodies of Suh and Kim until they were decapitated.[3]

It is rumored that Kim Jong Il also killed Kim Jung Wu, the former head of North Korea's External Economic Cooperation Promotion Committee, the "chief designer of the Rajin-Sonbong Economic Zone," and

Choe Hyon Tok, a member of the Foreign Affairs Committee of the Supreme People's Assembly.

Kim's brutal crackdown has effectively hushed political dissidents. Without outside military intervention, Kim Jong Il's government would more than likely sustain itself. But even the regime's collapse would not be as attractive as it sounds. As Andrew Natsios says: "The chaos resulting would threaten far more lives than those the famine has thus far claimed and could create an unpredictable military situation as well. Population movement to South Korea or China could prove explosive as both countries simultaneously take military measures to restore order, increasing the risk of conflict between them."[4]

South Korea does not want to see the fall of its "Berlin Wall." "After its financial crash in recent years, Seoul is less able than it was and less willing, to take on the burden of feeding North Korea. Therefore, South Korea is more likely than before to see its enemy — and brother — survive by muddling through."[5] The collapse of the Pyongyang regime will worsen South Korea's already difficult economy. This in turn will affect the Japanese economy, which is suffering from a decade of crisis. Neither of the two countries can help rebuild North Korea.

If the Pyongyang regime crumbles, the stability of China's border is threatened. The recent crackdown on North Korean escapees in Yanbian Korean Autonomous Prefecture showed China's determination to drive the "illegal immigrants" back to their country.

Today, the North Korean regime, although shaken, is still functioning and in control.

German doctor Norbert Vollertsen and his activists took affairs into their own hands when, in March 2002, they helped 25 North Koreans storm the Spanish Embassy in Beijing.

Doctor Vollertsen said: "We will create a flood of refugees to embassies, and it will lead to the collapse of North Korea. This is the way it happened in 1989, in Czechoslovakia and Hungary. First there were a few dozen defectors, then hundreds and then thousands."[6] In September 1989, in Prague, more than 1,100 East German defectors climbed over the fence of the West German Embassy. The historic events led to the collapse of the Berlin Wall.

However, almost immediately after the 25 North Koreans stormed into the Spanish Embassy in Beijing, witnesses in Yanbian Korean Autonomous Prefecture said that 150 uniformed North Korean agents, together with Chinese policemen, "are searching houses door to door, sweeping through construction sites, restaurants, markets, and inns. North Korean defectors hiding in Yanbian have been rounded up by North Korean security officials ... [and] many have been forced back across the border. The captives are sometimes badly beaten and kicked as they are hauled away. Arrested North Koreans are deported in truckloads several times a day. Some commit suicide by jumping from the bridge of the Yalu River."[7]

Around Yanji, the capital of Yanbian Korean Autonomous Prefecture, police order villagers to prepare for door-to-door ID checks and to report strangers. The search goes as far as Dalian in Liaoning Province and Beijing. The Chinese government will neither recognize the 300,000 North Korean escapees hiding in China as international refugees nor allow them to stay in China permanently. Brutal crackdowns will continue. Deportation is a daily matter. With tightened security and harsher punishment from both countries, a scenario of thousands storming into the South Korean Embassy in Beijing is nearly impossible. And the flooding of Western embassies is not likely to happen again in the near future.

24. The First Light

Is this the end of hope for the miserable North Korean people? Is there anything others in the world can do to help?

President Bush's critical stance toward Kim Jong Il's regime adds pressure for change. However, a tough policy alone will not work. The fact that North and South Korea are still enemies calls for a change in U.S. policy.

The United States should continue to engage North Korea: President Clinton's policy led to the summit between the two Koreas and several meetings between separated spouses. It was a step forward.

The policy of isolation and economic sanctions toward North Korea should be changed. The United States should help the North Korean government open up and quicken its economic reforms. The deaths of 3.5 million people have proved the failure of agricultural collectivization and planned economy in North Korea, as in other communist countries. But unlike China and the Soviet Union, where reforms were possible only after the deaths of Stalin and Mao, Kim Jong Il has already made up his mind to change. The numerous assassination attempts on his life have also forced him to think about his future and the future of his regime.

China's model adapts well to North Korea. At the beginning of its reforms during the late 1970's, China had just come out of the Cultural Revolution and stood at the verge of economic bankruptcy. At home, everything from rice to cooking oil was rationed. Developed countries shunned and isolated the mainland, depriving it of economic support. Today's North Korea holds many advantages over the China of that time. It has South Korea as its willing partner, and receives assistance from Japan, the United States, and China.

Kim Il Sung's failed Juche ideology has produced "a hungry army, a broken economy, widespread famine, and a challenge for the people of the world."[1] Inspired by China's successful economic reforms, Kim Jong Il will probably follow the lead of former Chinese leader Deng Xiaoping. Deng opposed Mao's philosophy by openly encouraging the Chinese people, who did not know what wealth meant at the end of the seventies, to get rich quickly. With the collapse of the ideological bondage of Juche, North Korea will learn to tolerate the political, social, and cultural freedoms that lead to economic reform.

The root of the severe food shortage in North Korea is the collective agricultural system, which provides farmers with no incentives to grow more grain because it rewards everyone equally, regardless of each individual's different abilities and efforts. The North Korean government should give the farmers freedom to grow and sell their own produce. When the peasants earn money, they will produce more grain to feed the cities. This in turn will fuel the rural economy and lead to a boom in the light industries because with money in hand, the peasants can consume. Heavy industry will follow and begin the cycle of trade.[2]

"If we continue to protect our own style of socialism, many more people will be killed under this rotten motto," a North Korean agricultural researcher concludes.

North Korea should seek better political relations with the West, specifically the United States, and with Japan and South Korea. The unstable political situation makes it difficult for large-scale foreign investment to enter North Korea. That investment is also prevented because of the extremely backward infrastructure. Factories, which lack spare parts and fuel, are on the verge of collapse. The country has few good transportation routes and no functional legal system. Unlike China, which has Taiwan, Hong Kong, Singapore, and a large population of overseas Chinese to support its economic reforms, North Korea does not have enough overseas Koreans to invest in the country, and its relations with South Korea are still in deadlock.

Kim Jong Il also has to overcome the strong resistance from hardliners, at various levels inside the Workers Party and the military, who are desperate to keep the status quo and protect their immediate interests. Kim should "find the best economic drivers and gradually free them from government constraints. Slowly, carefully abandon central planning by letting market forces grow within the country and then be influenced by the global economy."[3]

Although Kim has not yet altered his father's course in any meaningful way, change has begun. The North Korean government has established many special economic zones along the major railways. It has reopened the free economic zone at Rajin-Sunbong near the China border. In the early 1990's, the zone had already attracted foreign investment of over 100 million dollars before famine cut short the progress. The special economic zones provide the opportunity to pursue experiments that would further open up the country to foreign technology and investment. In 2001, South Korea's Hyundai Group obtained permission to set up an industrial park in the city of Kaesong. It plans to relocate from the South about 850 plants that make shoes, apparel, and other simple products. Many South Korean businesses want to take advantage of North Korea's cheap labor. In the economic zones, a North Korean worker is paid about $70 to $80 a month in a joint-ventured business. The salary is $100 for a totally foreign-run company.

The North Korean government also plans to develop Diamond Mountain and its vicinity into a tourist spot. At present, Diamond Mountain is the only place that South Koreans are allowed to visit in North Korea.

The initial results of the policy changes are apparent. In the past, North Korea could not make ready-to-eat noodles, but now it has its own name brand, the Daedong River. Using imported raw materials and technology, North Korea has started making textile products and musical instruments to be sold in foreign markets. It has also begun exporting laborers.[4]

North Korea has slackened control over foreign news coverage in the country. Before, it strictly restricted the number of Western reporters in the country and limited their coverage of major domestic activities. But after the summit meeting between the two Koreas in June 2000, North Korea readily allowed foreign journalists to report Russian president Putin's visit. When separated husbands and wives met in Pyongyang for the first time following the summit in 2000, North Korea permitted both Western and South Korean journalists to interview the spouses.

The Korean Central News Agency, mouthpiece of the Korean Workers Party, has also improved its news coverage by releasing one or two important news items on time and letting people know more about what is happening around them. However, the nature of news reporting in North Korea is still to withhold the truth for the Party's interests and propaganda purposes. "Public announcements are habitually characterized by deliberate deception,"[5] the former party secretary Hwang Jang-yop says.

In its 2002 evaluation of the present human-rights situation in North Korea, the U.S. State Department has admitted the improvement, even if in a negative way: "Although more foreign journalists, diplomats and representatives of humanitarian organizations have been allowed into the country, the Government still maintains the strictest control over the movements of foreign visitors." It complains that "journalists accompanying the U.S. Secretary of State in 2000 were not allowed to visit a department store or a train station; they were not allowed to talk to officials or to persons on the street. Those who arrived with cellular phones had them confiscated for the duration of their stay."[6]

The United Nations sees another positive sign since the Pyongyang Declaration in 2000. So far, exchange visits between families of the two Koreas have taken place on three occasions. American non-governmental organizations (NGOs) such as World Vision report that, although they still face difficult working conditions in North Korea, they have enjoyed better access to the hungry people than before. The World Food Program has opened four satellite offices throughout the country and food-aid monitors can visit almost all of North Korea. They also enjoy more say over the control of the food aid. To avoid government and military embezzlement, they ship food directly to smaller east coast ports for delivery inland. Also, by sending only barley and corn, which the Koreans do not like, those who are desperately hungry will get the grains, because the party elite and military want nothing but rice. Today, international food aid has successfully reduced the malnutrition rates among children under seven years old and improved their health.[7]

Under harsh criticism for its lack of human rights by people all over the world, the North Korean government has recently eased the punishment of defectors who are returned to the North. In the past a person who was caught stealing was publicly executed by a firing squad, but these days they are given jail terms. If the defectors escape to China solely out of starvation, they will be regarded as non-political prisoners and released shortly.

North Korea is promoting a whole new generation to important positions. While maintaining its traditional friendship with China and Russia, the government tries not to offend the United States. In the meantime, it further engages in economic exchange with other Western nations, particularly the European Union, to attract foreign capital and introduce new technology to the country.

On March 24, 2002, for the first time in history, North Korean Premier Hong Song Nam, in his report to the Supreme People's Assembly, called for economic reform and joint ventures with international businesses. The following are his (translated) words: "The main thrust of this year's economic construction is to make full preparations for technical improvement and modernization of the national economy as a whole, while readjusting the country's economic foundations in keeping with the practical demand."[8]

Kim Jong Il meeting with European leaders (Xiinhua News Agency).

To join the world market, Kim Jong Il, the only person who has the power to start the revolution, took bold steps in July 2002 to reintroduce cash into the economy: the government increased many workers' wages by 15 to 20 times. Military personnel and those who work for national defense industries see the biggest wage increases. Prices for almost everything have also risen about thirty times. As soon as the government announced that it has abandoned the food coupons, the price of food skyrocketed more than ten times. The price of rice, originally 0.80 won a kilogram, has gone up to 53 won, equal to a worker's half-month salary. Even so, shocked people scramble to buy and store rice, fearing another disastrous famine.

Free housing has become history. People who are not at all familiar with rent and utilities will have to pay for the first time in fifty years for their apartments. Using Korean won instead of revolutionary slogans to motivate workers, the government has also stopped supporting failing state-owned enterprises that are accustomed to getting free funds regardless of their productivity.[9]

These are just first moves towards a mixed economy of socialism and capitalism, a system Kim Jong Il so despised and condemned in the past.

With a better understanding of his North Korean counterpart than anyone else in the world, former South Korean President Kim Dae-jung believes that Kim Jong Il is now engaging in Chinese-style reforms and open-door policy. He believes Kim Jong Il is trying to turn North Korea into a second China. Kim Dae-jung even ordered the South Korean government to work out concrete plans to support North Korea's open-door policy.

"North Korea is expected to push through a considerable level of reforms and openness, so we must be prepared for that possibility," Kim told his cabinet members.

However, the process of reforming North Korea will not be fast. Rapid changes can cause Kim's regime to collapse and the country to be swallowed by South Korea. Rapid changes can lead to unexpected situations that Kim Jong Il cannot control, like those that happened in other former Communist countries.

Kim Jong Il does not want to be another Gorbechev in retirement, another Honecker in exile, or another Ceausescu hung from his palace balcony. To minimize the negative political impacts on his regime brought by the economic reforms, but also to realize a successful market economy in North Korea, Kim must reform cautiously, gradually, one area at a time to give himself plenty of room to stipulate, manipulate, and if necessary, to withdraw.[10] The whole process for Kim Jong Il to completely open up his country, as Kim Dae-jung predicted, will take at least twenty years.

The road to freedom and prosperity will not be easy. The miserable North Korean people, who work hard, love their families, value education and want a better life, will have to continue to endure more suffering and pay a high cost for the transition, even after a decade of deprivation. But changes are occurring, no matter how small and how reluctant they seem to be. The first light of bright horizons has already appeared.

All rivers flow into the sea. One day when I revisit North Korea, I hope to see happy people smiling, talking and laughing. They will live in new houses, travel in new cars on new networks of highways. Skyscrapers, department stores and supermarkets will dot every neighborhood. And food, mountains of food, will spill out of the markets. Women and children in their colorful traditional gowns will dance to the beat of the long drums while men wrestle in the park, the breeze of freedom gently touching their faces.

"When winter is here, can spring be too far away?"

I am waiting for the coming of North Korea's new spring.

I will open my arms to embrace the new country when flowers of liberty bloom on the once forbidden soil.

Appendix A: Timetable
of the Famine

- In the early 1990's, subsidized food and crude oil supplies from the Soviet Union and China are reduced.
- In 1991, the Kim Il Sung regime calls for a two-meal-a-day campaign to ration diminishing food supplies.
- In 1992, food distributions become intermittent in the northeast prefectures.
- In October 1993, the framework agreement eases nuclear tensions and opens door for international food assistance.
- In July 1994, Kim Il Sung dies and Kim Jong Il ascends to power.
- In 1994, Kim Jong Il regime shuts down the public food distribution system in the northeast prefectures.
- In August 1994, massive flooding occurs throughout the country.
- In September 1994, the Kim Jong Il regime reduces grain rations for rural families.
- In April 1995, North Korea agrees to join the U.S., China, and South Korea in Four-Party Peace Talks.
- In late 1995, Kim Jong Il thwarts a reported military coup in the northeast prefectures.
- In 1996, the Kim Jong Il regime moves responsibility for managing the food-distribution system from national to county authorities.

- Selective food distribution continues in the capital. Party cadres, workers from critical industries, and the military continue to receive rations.
- In early 1997, famine peaks. There are unconfirmed reports of martial law.
- In January 1997, drought occurs across agricultural areas. The Kim Jong Il regime announces that families are now responsible for feeding themselves.
- In February 1997, Kim Dae-jung is inaugurated as President of South Korea. He initiates "Sunshine Policy" seeking North-South reconciliation.
- On September 27, 1997, Kim Jong Il creates 927 detention camps throughout the country for internally displaced people caught without travel permits.
- In spring 1998, food prices in private markets decrease due to influx of international food aid shipments.
- In summer 1998, Kim Jong Il tightens travel-permit regulations and imposes new fines to re-establish order after a period of population movement while searching for food. Purchases of Chinese corn decline because of production decline, thereby increasing the price of grain in private markets.

Chapter Notes

The citation "refugee testimonies, *Chosun Journal*" refers to the web site www.chosunjournal.com, where one can click on "testimonies" to find personal stories of North Korean refugees. The citation "testimonies of North Korean defectors, New Millennium" refers to the web site of the National Intelligence Service, *New Millennium* (www.nis.go.kr/eng/).

1. The Yalu River

1. "Deadly Drought," by *Northern China Daily News*, June 5, 2000.

3. The Travel Guards

1. "Development in Korean Peninsular," *Communication Inside the Party* Issue 17, 2000.
2. "North Korean Food Relief Called Not Enough," *Atlanta Constitution*, February 11, 2002.
3. Kim Kwang-in, "Pyongyang College of Foreign Languages Allows Escape from 'Closed Society,'" *Chosun Journal*, March 2002.
4. *Communication Inside the Party* (Shanghai), Issue 20, 2001.
5. *Jiangnan Evening News*, March 10, 2001.

4. On Route to Mt. Myohyang

1. People's News Agency, Denmark, 1997. Reprinted with permission of People's News Agency, Plantanvej 30, 1810 Frederiksberg C, Denmark, gtimes@post8.tele.dk.
2. Kim Il Sung, *On Juche in Our Revolution* (New York: Weekly Guardian Associates), page 167.
3. Refugee testimonies, *Chosun Journal*.
4. Interview with authors in Yanbian.

5. Kim Il Sung, God in North Korea

1. Refugee testimonies, *Chosun Journal.*
2. U.S. Department of State, *Democratic People's Republic of Korea Country Report on Human Rights Practices for 2002*, released by the Bureau of Democracy, Human Rights, and Labor, February 26, 2002.
3. Hazel Smith, "Desperate Times in North Korea: Power Cuts and Food Shortage Make Life Hard in Pyongyang," *Far Eastern Economic Review*, February 14, 2002.
4. U.S. Department of State, *Democratic People's Republic of Korea Country Report on Human Rights Practices for 2002*, released by the Bureau of Democracy, Human Rights, and Labor, February 26, 2002.
5. Bruce Comings, *Korea's Place in the Sun* (New York: Norton, 1998) page 407.
6. U.S. Department of State, *Democratic People's Republic of Korea Country Report on Human Rights Practices for 2002*, released by the Bureau of Democracy, Human Rights, and Labor, February 26, 2002.

6. Kim Jong Il Behind the Veil

1. "Hwang Jang-yop Speaks," testimonies of North Korean defectors, *New Millennium.*
2. People's News Agency, Denmark, 1997. Reprinted with permission of People's News Agency, Plantanvej 30, 1810 Frederiksberg C, Denmark, gtimes@post8.tele.dk.
3. "Mysterious Ruler: Kim Jong Il," *New Century News*, January 24, 2003.
4. Donald Macintyre, "The Supremo in His Labyrinth," *Choongang Monthly Magazine*, February 18, 2002.
5. Kim Mi-young, "Secret Farm Feeds Pyongyang's Elite," *Chosun Journal*, May 2001.
6. Riona Terry, "Feeding the Dear Leader," *The Italian Guardian*, August 2001.
7. "Kim's Train Is Like a Five-Star Hotel," World Journal, August 6, 2001.
8. "Kim Jong Il's Train Trip to Russia," *Global News*, July 31, 2001.
9. "Kim's Eldest Son," *Jiangnan Evening News*, December 28, 2000.
10. Kim Kwang-in, "Body Guards of Kim Jong Il," *Chosun Journal*, May 2001.
11. Kim Kwang-in, "Body Guards of Kim Jong Il," *Chosun Journal*, May 2001.
12. "The Real North Korea," *Features* (Beijing), Issue 30, 2001.
13. "Hwang Jang-yop Speaks," testimonies of North Korean defectors, New Millennium.

7. Pyongyang — Hell and Paradise

1. *Communications Inside the Party*, (Shanghai), Issue 25, 2001.
2. Interview with the authors.
3. Consular Information Sheet, U.S. Government, June 21, 2001.
4. U.S. Department of State, *Democratic People's Republic of Korea Coun-*

try Report on Human Rights Practices for 2002, released by the Bureau of Democracy, Human Rights, and Labor, February 26, 2002.

5. "Kang Hyeok Hospital Experience," refugee testimonies, *Chosun Journal*.

6. "North Korea's Elite Need Their Starbucks and TVs," Reuters, April 1, 2002.

8. In the Shadow of Juche

1. Zhang Jifan, "Get Close to North Korea," *Writer's Forum* (Beijing), March 23, 2001.

2. Jasper Becker, *South China Morning Post*, June 17, 2001.

3. "What Are the North Korean Youths Doing?" *Digest News* (Shanghai), March 5, 2001.

9. Pyongyang's Everyday Life

1. Simon Bone, "My Trip to North Korea," September 1998. See Bone's web site, www.simonbone.com.

2. "Life in Pyongyang Apartments," JoongAng Ilbo, 2001.

3. U.S. Department of State, Democratic People's Republic of Korea Country Report on Human Rights Practices for 2002, released by the Bureau of Democracy, Human Rights, and Labor, February 26, 2002

4. "Hwang Jang-yop Speaks," testimonies of North Korean defectors, *New Millennium*.

10. Underground Casino

1. U.S. Department of State, *Democratic People's Republic of Korea Country Report on Human Rights Practices for 2002*, released by the Bureau of Democracy, Human Rights, and Labor, February 26, 2002.

2. Jasper Becker, *Hungry Ghosts*: Mao's Secret Famine (New York: Free Press, 1997), page 315.

3. U.S. Department of State, *Democratic People's Republic of Korea Country Report on Human Rights Practices for 2002*, released by the Bureau of Democracy, Human Rights, and Labor, February 26, 2002.

4. James Pringle, "North Korea Unbends to Allow E-mail Service," *Digital Chosun Journal*, 2001.

5. Kim Mi-young, "No Objective Tests for North Korean Students," *Chosun Journal*, March 2001.

6. U.S. Department of State, *Democratic People's Republic of Korea Country Report on Human Rights Practices for 2002*, released by the Bureau of Democracy, Human Rights, and Labor, February 26, 2002.

11. The DMZ

1. "Hwang Jang-yop Speaks," testimonies of North Korean defectors, *New Millennium*.

2. People's News Agency, Denmark, 1997. Reprinted with permission of People's News Agency, Plantanvej 30, 1810 Frederiksberg C, Denmark, gtimes@post8.tele.dk.

3. "Hwang Jang-yop Speaks," testimonies of North Korean defectors, *New Millennium.*

4. John E. McLaughlin, "North Korea, Engagement or Confrontation," address delivered to Texas A & M Conference, April 17, 2001.

5. "Marshal Peng De Huai in Korean War," *Writer's Forum*, June 20, 2000.

6. Wang Shu Zeng, "The War in the Far East," *Writer's Forum*, July 4, 2000.

7. "Korean War," *Writer's Forum*, March 23, 2001.

8. Kim Kwang-in, "Life in the North Korean Army," *Chosun Journal.*

9. "NK Bio-Weapons Are Everyone's Business," *Chosun Journal*, March 23, 2002.

10. Richard Burns, "Rumsfeld: Potentially Deadly Link Between Networks and 'Terrorist States' Must Be Stopped," Associated Press, February 1, 2002.

11. "A Japanese Professor Says That the North Korean Government Orders Its Military Personnel to Engage in Terrorist Operations Abroad on the Cheap," Forbes.com, September 26, 2001.

12. Soon-Sung Cho, *The Korean War Almanac* (New York: Facts on File, 1990), page 353.

13. Andrew Ward, "Gunfire Underlines Strain Between Two Koreas," Associated Press, November 2001.

14. Zhang Xin Hua, "The Potato Revolution in North Korea," *Everyone's Weekly*, December 23, 2000.

15. "The Government Encourages Goat Raising," *JoongAng Ilbo*, 2001.

16. "*The Government Encourages Goat Raising*," *JoongAng Ilbo*, 2001.

12. Out of the Prison Country

1. "Hwang Jang-yop Speaks," testimonies of North Korean defectors, *New Millennium.*

2. "Bush says North Koreans Unaware of U.S. Food Aid, *Chosun Journal*, February 28, 2002.

3. Kang Hyeok, refugee testimonies, *Chosun Journal.*

13. Massive Flight

1. Jasper Becker, Hungry Ghosts: Mao's Secret Famine (New York: Free Press, 1997), page 339.

2. U.S. Department of State, *Democratic People's Republic of Korea Country Report on Human Rights Practices for 2002*, released by the Bureau of Democracy, Human Rights, and Labor, February 26, 2002.

3. Kim Chol-hwan, "Housewives Make Handsome Profits in Cross-border Smuggling," *Chosun Journal*, June 2001.

4. Kim Chol-hwan, "Housewives Make Handsome Profits in Cross-border Smuggling," *Chosun Journal*, June 2001.

14. Cold Water Village

1. U.S. Department of State, *Democratic People's Republic of Korea Country Report on Human Rights Practices for 2002*, released by the Bureau of Democracy, Human Rights, and Labor, February 26, 2002.

2. John Pomfret, "China Steps Up Repatriation of North Korean Refugees," *Washington Post Foreign Service*, July 23, 2001.

3. According to the office of the United Nations High Commissioner of Refugees, throughout the world today there are about twenty million refugees. Under the international human rights regime, the country of first refuge is required to accept refugees temporarily, until they can return to their countries or find a new home in some country. (This is an expanded version of an article which appeared in *China Rights Forum*, Summer/Fall 2000).

4. "Chinese Premier Zhu Rongjia Agreed on North Korean...," Associated Press, March 14, 2002.

15. The Dangerous Life of the Escapee

1. In addition to author interviews, the chapter also draws on other refugee testimonies.

16. Young Victims

1. Kang Chol-hwan, *The Aquariums of Pyongyang* (New York: Basic, 2002), page 146.

2. Kang Chol-hwan, *The Aquariums of Pyongyang* (New York: Basic, 2002), page 146.

3. Central Intelligence Agency, *World Factbook* (www.cia.gov/cia/publications/factbook/index.html).

4. Antoaneta Bezlova, "About 80000 Children on the Verge of Starvation," Associated Press, Beijing, July 2, 2001.

5. Refugee testimonies, *Chosun Journal*.

6. Refugee testimonies, *Chosun Journal*.

7. Kang Chol-hwan, *The Aquariums of Pyongyang* (New York: Basic, 2002), pages 139–141.

8. Kang Hyeok, refugee testimonies, Chosun Journal.

17. North Korea's Auschwitz

1. Kang Chol-hwan, *The Aquariums of Pyongyang*, pages 139–141.

2. In addition to author interviews, the chapter also draws on several other refugee testimonies from *Chosun Journal*.

18. The Mongolia Route

1. Li Da, "Thousands are Fleeing from North Korea," *News Around the World*, Jan 15, 1999.

2. "Hwang Jang-yop Speaks," *testimonies of North Korean defectors, New Millennium*.

3. "Flee to China," *Mid-US Times*, June 2000.

4. David Rennie, "Terror Faces Starving Who Flee to China," *Christian Science Monitor*, January 9, 2001.

5. Jasper Becker, *South China Morning Post*, June 17, 2001.
6. "Escape to the South," *The Economist*, February 14, 2001.

19. Seeking a Change

1. Andrew Natsios, *Report on Current North Korea* (United States Institute of Peace, 1998). This report analyzes the North Korean food crisis, which began in 1994 and evolved into a major famine with high death rates. The report considers the causes of the famine, the central government's response to it, and the popular reaction to the government's inability to stem the steady collapse of the old system, as well as the convulsive effects of the famine on North Korean society, political system, and military. The international humanitarian aid response to the famine has had the unintended affect of weakening the central government's control over the society and has stimulated irrevocable changes in the economy. The report argues that much of the regime's external behavior is driven by the famine and considers the implications of the famine for the future of the country.

2. Sue Lautze, Independent food observer to the PRC & DPRK, Final Report, June 1996.

3. Hwang Jang-yop, *Truth or Lies*, page 15.

4. Andrew Natsios, *Report on Current North Korea* (United States Institute of Peace, 1998.

5. Fu Suo-chang, "Kim Jong Il, the General Designer for North Korea's Economic Reforms," *Writer's Forum*, January 19, 2001.

6. "Hwang Jang-yop Speaks," testimonies of North Korean defectors, *New Millennium*.

7. "Kim Jong Il's Reform," *China's Military Newspaper*, May 8, 2001.

8. "North Korea's Experimental Open-up," *Communication Inside the Party* (Shanghai), Issue 22, 2000.

9. "North Korea's Experimental Open-up," *Communication Inside the Party* (Shanghai), Issue 22, 2000.

10. James Conachy, "China Pushes North Korea to Accelerate Free Market Policies," World Socialist Web Site, February 6, 2001.

11. *Communication Inside the Party* (Shanghai), Issue 18, 2000.

20. Engaging the West

1. "Hwang Jang-yop Speaks," testimonies of North Korean defectors, *New Millennium*.

2. People's News Agency, Demark, 1997. Reprinted with permission of People's News Agency, Plantanvej 30, 1810 Frederiksberg C, Denmark, gtimes@post8.tele.dk.

3. "Hwang Jang-yop Speaks," testimonies of North Korean defectors, *New Millennium*.

4. Roger Barrett of the Foreign Business Development Association.

5. Miles Benson, "U.S. Blamed in North Korea Crisis," Newhouse News Service, November 17, 2002.

6. Miles Benson, "U.S. Blamed in North Korea Crisis," Newhouse News Service, November 17, 2002.

7. Howard W. French, "North Korea Restarts Nuclear Program," *New York Times*, December 13, 2002.

8. Oh Young-jin, "Majority of Americans Support Dialog with N. Korea: Survey," *Chosun Journal*.

21. Beautifying Terrorism

1. Sachiko Sakamaki, "Japanese Family Is Told Daughter was Abducted," *Washington Post*, December, 2002.

2. Lee Young-jong, "North Korean Defectors Missing," *Chosun Journal*, February 15, 2002.

3. Lee Kyo-kwan, "Fate of Ex-head of Economic Cooperation Committee a Mystery," *Chosun Journal*.

4. People's News Agency, Denmark, 1997. Reprinted with permission of People's News Agency, Plantanvej 30, 1810 Frederiksberg C, Denmark, gtimes@post8.tele.dk.

5. Alexander G. Higgins: "The leader of long-reclusive North Korea said he would open ties with the United States right away if it removes his country from a list of terrorism-sponsoring nations, South Korea's state media reported Sunday." Associated Press, August 14, 2000.

22. Starve the Regime to Death?

1. "North Korea: UN Food Agency's Biggest Operation Worldwide ROME, Italy, October 22, 2001 (ENS)— The United Nations World Food Programme today said it is rushing emergency rations to tens of thousands of flood victims in the Democratic People's Republic of Korea (DPRK), following freak rains in the southeast of the country that caused massive damage to crops, homes and roads and bridges. Eighty-one people were killed, 33 people are missing, and 84 were seriously injured."

2. Andrew Natsios, Refugee interviews, September 1998.

3. Bruce Comings, *Korea's Place in the Sun* (New York: Norton, 1998), page 494.

4. Andrew Gregorovich, "Black Famine in Ukraine," *FORUM Ukrainian Review* No. 24, 1974.

5. Arthur Koestler, "The God That Failed," *FORUM Ukrainian Review* No. 24, 1974.

6. Andrew Gregorovich, "Black Famine in Ukraine," *FORUM Ukrainian Review* No. 24, 1974.

7. Jin Fu, *Ten Years Before the Cultural Revolution* (Beijing: Chinese Communist Party College, 1998), page 196.

8. Jasper Becker, Hungry Ghost, 1997, page 338.

9. Between 1997 to 1998, the KBSM's interviews of 1,679 food refugees in China's Yan Bian confirmed that famine occurred first in urban and mining areas. In some maize-growing mountainous areas, death rate is as high as 26 to 28 percent among miners and city dwellers.

10. Hwang Jang-yop, *Truth or Lies*, Chapter 20, page 15.

11. Jasper Becker, *Hungry Ghosts: Mao's Secret Famine* (New York: Free Press, 1997), page 339.

23. Rise in Arms?

1. Refugee testimonies, *Chosun Journal*.

2. U.S. Department of State, *Democratic People's Republic of Korea Country Report on Human Rights Practices for 2002*, released by the Bureau of Democracy, Human Rights, and Labor, February 26, 2002.

3. Refugee testimonies, *Chosun Journal*.

4. Andrew Natsios, "Report on Current North Korea" (United States Institute of Peace, 1998).

5. Bruce Comings, *Korea's Place in the Sun* (New York: Norton, 1998), page 495.

6. Barbara Demick, "Activists Promise Flood of Refugees from North Korea," *Los Angeles Times*, March 19, 2002.

7. John Leicester, "China Confirms Crack Down on Koreans," Associated Press, March 25, 2002.

24. The First Light

1. John E. McLaughlin, "North Korean, Engagement or Confrontation," address delivered to Texas A&M Conference, April 17, 2001.

2. Michael Parks and Gregory F. Treverton, "North Korea Considers 'Going Chinese,'" *Los Angeles Times*, January 26, 2001.

3. Michael Parks and Gregory F. Treverton, "North Korea Considers 'Going Chinese,'" *Los Angeles Times*, January 26, 2001.

4. Fu Suo-chang, "Kim Jong Il, the General Designer for North Korea's Economic Reforms," *Writer's Forum*, January 19, 2001.

5. "Hwang Jang-yop Speaks," testimonies of North Korean defectors, *New Millennium*.

6. U.S. Department of State, *Democratic People's Republic of Korea Country Report on Human Rights Practices for 2002*, released by the Bureau of Democracy, Human Rights, and Labor, February 26, 2002.

7. "NGOS Support Additional Emergency Food Shipments to North Korea," Statement by Adventist Development and Relief Agency, American Friends Service Committee, CARE, Church World Service, Holt International Children's Services, Institute for Strategic Reconciliation, Korean-American Sharing Movement, Mennonite Central Committee, Mercy Corps International, Oxfam/America, World Vision, September 25, 2001. American NGOs assisting the people of North Korea issued a statement September 25 supporting the administration's decision to provide an additional 300,000 metric tons of food aid. The signatory agencies are members of the NGO Working Group on North Korea organized and supported by InterAction.

8. "North Korea to Open Its Door, Staff and Wires," *Chosun Journal*, March 27, 2002.

9. "The Economic Changes Start Cautiously in North Korea," *Global News*, August 5, 2002.

10. John E. McLaughlin, "North Korea, Engagement or Confrontation," address delivered to Texas A & M Conference, April 17, 2001.

Appendix

1. Andrew Natsios, *Report on Current North Korea*, (United States Institute of Peace, 1998).

Index